MY *American* DREAM

ONE WOMAN'S JOURNEY
LIVING WITH A CHRONIC DISEASE

DR. MARIA MILLER

Copyright © 2022 Dr. Maria Miller.

All rights reserved. No part of this book may be reproduced, stored, or transmitted by any means—whether auditory, graphic, mechanical, or electronic—without written permission of both publisher and author, except in the case of brief excerpts used in critical articles and reviews. Unauthorized reproduction of any part of this work is illegal and is punishable by law.

ISBN: 979-8-88640-226-1 (sc)
ISBN: 979-8-88640-227-8 (hc)
ISBN: 979-8-88640-228-5 (e)

Because of the dynamic nature of the Internet, any web addresses or links contained in this book may have changed since publication and may no longer be valid. The views expressed in this work are solely those of the author and do not necessarily reflect the views of the publisher, and the publisher hereby disclaims any responsibility for them.

One Galleria Blvd., Suite 1900, Metairie, LA 70001
1-888-421-2397

I would first like to thank God, in Him I have found the strength and the courage that has helped me find peace in my life. I would also like to thank my parents for always believing in me, and setting an example of hard work, dedication and perseverance. I would like to thank my Husband. We have traveled through life together, and he has always been by my side through thick and thin. I would like to thank my children for inspiring me and giving me purpose. Last, I would like to thank all of the parents and their children who I have had the privilege of seeing and caring for throughout my career. Thank you for being a part of my life, and thank you for allowing me to be a part of your family.

Thank you to Pamela Philpott for editing the manuscript, and to John Weis for consulting on this project.

PROLOGUE

All factual information that follows regarding rheumatoid arthritis, its symptoms, causes and side affects was obtained from WebMD at www.webmd.com.

Rheumatoid arthritis (RA) is a type of chronic arthritis that typically occurs symmetrically in the joints of the body, for example RA would not affect the hands, feet, knees or fingers on one side of the body. Whatever joint grouping affected by this disease would be equally affected on both the right and left side of the afflicted person's anatomy.

I write to tell you about RA in the beginning of my book not to discourage, nor to solicit any pity from anyone who may be reading. I am a woman, I am a mother, I am a wife, and I have RA. This disease has been both a blessing and a challenge throughout my life. What follows this prologue is, hopefully, an inspirational tale of a little girl born in a small farming village in Spain, who grew up to be a successful physician living her dream in the United State of America, all the while suffering from RA.

This illness is characterized by redness, warmth, swelling and pain within the joint. It is a chronic illness, which means that there is no timeframe for which the illness lasts. It is a life-long battle after the onset of the first symptoms.

On top of the many joint-related issues that can be attributed to the disease, RA may affect other areas of the human anatomy. These areas include, but are not limited to, the skin, eyes, lungs, heart, blood, and the body's nervous system.

This disease can present in many different manifestations. For some the disease can progress gradually over several years, for others the disease's onset may be sudden and dramatic. There is a fraction of the population that may have "flare ups" of the disease and then regress into a stage of remission where symptoms are not noticeable, but the disease, nonetheless, is still and always will be a part of their lives.

RA is a disease that affects nearly one percent of the U.S. population, but is two to three times more likely to manifest itself in women than in men. The disease usually first presents in middle age; however, it is not limited to this age group.

The disease itself is quite mysterious and, still to this day, is not fully understood. Although incidences of the disease have been documented throughout history, with some scholars dating the initial traces to around 4500 B.C., there is still no concrete explanation as to why or how it arises.

The disease itself is triggered by the body's immune system, causing immune cells to migrate from the blood into the joints, and the joint lining tissue, called the synovium. Once in the synovium, the immune cells produce inflammatory substances within the joint causing irritations, a wearing down of the cartilage, and swelling and inflammation of the joint lining. When the lining is inflamed excessive joint fluid is produced, As a result, the cartilage within the joint is worn down, and the space between the bones narrows. To further exacerbate the situation as the joint lining expands, it can invade or erode the adjacent bone, resulting in bone damage commonly known as bone erosion. All of these factors result in the joint becoming very painful, swollen, and warm to the touch.

With all of the physiology that we know of this disease, its origin is still a mystery. There is a combination of theories out there to suggest that genetic, environmental, and hormonal factors could all play a role in the presentation of RA.

There are other theories that suggest a virus or bacteria may alter the immune system, causing it to attack the joints. There are even more theories that suggest smoking may play a part in causing or contributing to the onset of RA. With all of the research and medical breakthroughs that have occurred, a single reputable link to the causation of this painful disease has not been established.

Besides the visible symptoms that include stiffness, pain, swelling, and reddening of the skin, RA also affects other parts of the body, as well as the mind. Sufferers of this disease have reported fatigue, loss of appetite, muscle aches, and a general feeling of illness.

Consequently, the disease also plays an active role as a contributor to lung issues due to fluid build up, as well as heart conditions. Studies have shown RA sufferers to be twice as likely as others to develop heart illness. In some rare cases, RA can even affect the eyes, leading to complications that may ultimately lead to vision loss.

Another consequence of this chronic illness is that it takes a toll on the individual's outward appearance. Rheumatoid nodules can develop underneath a person's skin and develop near the person's affected joints.

Rheumatoid nodules are firm, flesh-colored lumps that grow under the skin, and can be either as large as a walnut or as small as a pea. They typically cause no pain, but in rare cases, where nerves are pressured or organs are affected, they may lead to complications.

Rheumatoid nodules, as well as forms of deformity in the joints, are a serious consequence of the illness. When the illness presents itself in the joints of the hands and fingers, deformities are likely to arise. One particular form of deformity is the swan neck. It is estimated that half of those who suffer from RA have this type of deformity, which is characterized by the base of the finger and the outermost joint bending, while the middle joint straightens. Over time, the imbalance in the joints causes the crooked swan-neck position of the hand.

RA is a painful disease, physically because of the brutality inflicted on the affected joints and mentally because it disproportionately preys on females. It affects a person's outward appearance, which can also lead to self-image questions and, eventually, depression.

Studies have shown that approximately 11 percent of people living with RA have or had symptoms of moderately severe to severe depression. The people studied indicated the restriction on normal life activities as the top reason for their prolonged sense of depression. RA is a tough disease and a struggle that those who suffer from it from must endure every single day of their lives. These brave individuals must undergo countless treatments, rounds of medications and drugs, and the uncertainty of why they, out of millions of people, inexplicably have had to endure such a hardship in their lives.

My story is meant to inspire women, especially Latin women like myself, to understand that we can make a difference, and we should make a difference. I have lived in this country for almost 30 years, and through that time I have prospered and succeeded where, at first glance, things seemed mighty bleak. We are at a time in our society where things are looking bleak once more, but it is up to us as a society to pick ourselves up, dust ourselves off and inspire our people to greatness once more.

I have lived with a debilitating disease for most of my life, I have persevered, and I have achieved what I believe to be success. I know that there are many others out there who could do the same and more, if only they had the right chance and inspiration. I hope this book brings hope, joy and inspiration to all of those who read it, because it brings me joy to present it to you. I am proud of it, and I am proud of sharing my life story with all of you. I hope everyone can find a little piece of me in them, and I hope that you are encouraged to follow your dreams, like I did, in spite of any obstacles that may lie in your way.

Dr. Maria Luisa Miller

CHAPTER 1

> "Imagination will often carry us to worlds
> that never were. But without it we go nowhere."
> —*CARL SAGAN*

Sabuz, Spain, is a tiny farming village in the northwest corner of the Iberian Peninsula. It is located in the region commonly referred to as Galicia. This tiny farming village was home to approximately 100 to 200 people in 1954. The country was only recently recovering from a long and bloody civil war, people were hungry and jobs were scarce. To make matters worse, education was not exactly a top priority in the lives of those in this farming community.

Most people were subsistence farmers growing what they needed on plots of land that had been handed down through generations, or trading crops and livestock for food and necessary goods. Life was hard, and times were difficult, but the people survived. The generation entering adulthood had difficult decisions to make. Should they marry? If so, then how were they supposed to support their spouse? With no work in the foreseeable future, how would they support a family? Would they even be able to house and shelter a family? What sort of future could they provide to their offspring without any opportunity or stability?

It was these questions that wreaked havoc on the minds of the young men and women of 1950s Spain. In the midst of all of these troubling times, the simple people continued to ply their trade, growing crops for sustenance and raising livestock for survival.

These types of tiny enclaves were typical of all of Spain at the time. The villages were tight-knit communities where each family blurred into extended distortions of itself. There was no crime, and it was unheard of for people to lock doors or shutter themselves inside of the home at night. The simplicity of life really made one appreciate the beauty of community.

Sabuz is really unremarkable from any other Spanish farming village save for the fact that it was the place where I was born. On May 10, 1955, I, Dr. Maria Luisa Miller, was born in this small farming community – the first child of Sra. Dolores Rodriguez Ferro and Sr. Emilio Ferro.

My parents were simple people, and I mean that with all due respect. They came from a different time and a different place. Their values placed a premium on hard work and achievement through sweat and force. They were farmers who were the children of farmers.

My father was born in a nearby town named Freijoso, also in Galicia, Spain. He was one of nine brothers and sisters. His father died when he was only four years old, leaving his mother to raise nine children. In his household, the chores were divided; some children were charged with inside chores, while others helped maintain the family's land. My father was one of those chosen to work the fields. He grew up accomplishing back-breaking work outdoors with his only satisfaction being the knowledge that he was doing his part to help his mother keep the family together.

My mother was born in Sabuz. She was one of four children born to Dolores Rodriguez and Celso Rodriguez. At the age of 18, she married my father, Emilio Ferro, and they settled in Sabuz. I came along when my mother was age 20.

Faced with the grim reality of a growing family, and very little in the way of supporting said brood, my father was forced to make a very difficult decision. He was limited in his options in the arena of employment. Except for a brief stint in a seminary school where he learned to read and write, he had no real formal education. My mother never learned how to read or to write. They were equipped with only the tools for manual labor, and blue-collar chores, but there was no future in the country for those types of jobs.

My father was forced to emigrate from his homeland in order to find ways to support his now growing family. How was he to do this? Where was he to go to finance such an expedition, and who was going to support him and his family while he searched for work overseas? He went to the only person he knew who would support him in his decision to leave the country. He approached his mother, who had encouraged all of her children to go in search of a better life elsewhere, and asked her for her financial support. She was not a woman of means, but whatever she had she was more than willing to share with her children as long as it was to improve their lives. With that said, she sold whatever livestock and furniture she had, and she financed his adventure in search of a better life.

But who was to care for my mother and me? This question laid the foundation for the first seven years of my life, and is how I developed a special bond with my grandfather that has never been and will never be duplicated with anyone. My mother's parents cared for us while my father searched for a better life. They housed me, fed me and loved me as their own.

When I was two months old, my father left Spain in search of work and progress overseas. At first he went to Santo Domingo in the Dominican Republic, but he was met with more struggles and little success there. He next moved on to Venezuela in South America, where he would eventually settle and send for my mother a few years later.

From infancy through my toddler years all the way up to age seven, the only memories I have of my father are those generated from letters, pictures, and stories people in the town would tell me. He never returned to Spain. When I was four years old, my father was able to send for my mother and move her to Venezuela to help him with work and savings. The idea was to save up enough money, so that they could eventually take me over to join them there. Although this may seem out of the ordinary and peculiar to people, this was all that I knew. This was my normal.

I had a loving home provided by my grandparents, and I had parents, just not the garden-variety type. My grandfather was fiercely protective of his family, and I rather liked having him wrapped around my finger as his only granddaughter.

Times were tough, but how tough could they really be? I mean, after all we were just a small farming village in the northwest of Spain. Well, for my mother, life with regards to me was pretty difficult. For example, medical care was not at the forefront of technology in Sabuz at the time. There was no doctor or hospital in the town, which made childbirth a challenge and a dangerous event. For this process, women were forced to give birth at home with no medical supervision, and only family and friends around for support and care. My birth was no different from any other, and so I entered this world like all of the children in my village, born in my parents' home in Sabuz.

Luckily for me, everything went as smooth as can be on that end. I'm not saying that it was a pleasurable time for my mother, but I came out of the ordeal relatively unscathed. She, on the other hand, may have had some different comments to make with regard to the whole birth-without-unaesthetic thing, but I digress.

I mention this fact because it lays the foundation for the first brush that I had with medicine as a child. When I was two years old I became very ill. I have no memory of this time, and that is probably for the better. As it was later retold to me, I was a relatively calm baby and didn't need much special attention. When I needed to be fed, I was fed, when I needed to be changed I was changed, but for the most part I was a simple and happy child.

That all changed when I became two years old. One night, I suddenly became insufferable, I would cry and weep in my bed, and I ran an uncontrollable fever. No matter what my mother and grandparents tried, they could not get this illness under control. Things went on like this for days, and there seemed to be no end to any of the symptoms. It got to a point where my family feared the worst. They thought that I had contracted some sort of disease, and that it would invariably take my life. Here, my mother was 22 years old, her husband was living in Venezuela sending back what he could to help, and there was no medical attention anywhere in sight.

She decided that she could not take this anymore and, if there was nothing else she could do, at least she was going to get me to a doctor so that they could diagnose the problem and give her a solution. She was prepared to hear the worst news possible, as long as she knew that she had not just sat around and waited for the inevitable, as it was in their minds.

She saw that her child was suffering, and she wanted to rid herself of this feeling of hopelessness. Finally, a few nights later in a driving storm, she bundled me up, packed my things, and headed out for the nearest town that had some form of medical care.

The nearest place with a clinic was an hour's walk away in a town called Cartelle. Cartelle was by no means a thriving metropolis. It was a town with a population of about 2,000 at the time. What it did have was doctors and a medical clinic, and, hopefully, an answer for my mother as to why her young daughter was so sick. So, off she went in the middle of the night in a driving storm for an hour's walk and, hopefully, some resolution to my illness.

Once she arrived in Cartelle, I was seen and the doctor who saw me diagnosed me with the measles. Today, the measles is a virtually extinct illness that we have all but eradicated through vaccination, but at the time I had had no contact with any sort of vaccine for this illness.

After the diagnosis, the doctor treated me, and eventually I recovered, but had it not been for my mother's determination and insistence on not standing by idly as this virus ravaged her child, things could have turned out very differently for me.

Life returned back to normal at our home. My grandfather decided to sell everything in Sabuz and move to Sarreaus, another small farming community near the Portugal border in Orense, and not far from Sabuz and Bande. I don't know why he did this, but, as a child, you learn not to ask many questions and just go with the flow. People were still depressed due to the fact that there were no jobs or money. Education was still not a priority, because reading books doesn't pay the bills, and the lack of economic prosperity really began to take its toll on the population of these tiny villages.

My first memory that I can vividly recall is really a great indicator of how things were in those times. I was three years old. It was a cold night, and I was asleep all tucked in and cozy in bed at my grandparent's house. Suddenly, the door swung open and in walked my mother. Startled, I jumped up in bed, and asked her if everything was OK. She told me to get out of bed and put my shoes on because we had to look for a neighbor who had gone missing earlier in the day. I did as I was told, and when I came outside nearly the entire village had gathered in search of this gentleman. We searched all over the village looking for this man. I could remember flashlights and kerosene lanterns swaying back and forth at all points of the town. People were screaming his name, with me joining in, not really understanding what was going on. Soon enough, though, I would understand.

We searched for what seemed was hours, but in reality probably wasn't all that long, before we made the gruesome discovery. After reaching a clearing in some fields and stumbling upon an area with some high-grown trees, there he was, the man for whom we were searching. Apparently, this man had been enduring some tough times. He had been feeling the stress of the economy and was unable to bear the weight of the country's instability that seemed to be never ending. The whole town gathered around, and before anyone could warn the children to look away, or shield them from the sight, this man's lifeless body was clearly visible swinging high in the wind, hanging from a tree.

That image is so ingrained in my mind for several reasons. First and foremost was that it was a horrific sight. Death is not something to fear, but when placed face to face with it at such a young age one must ask if this traumatic experience was something that may have shaped one's outlook and perspective on life in general. Second, it was symbolical of the times. Here was a man who, for all intents and purposes, was a good person. I'd never really known the man, but he was good enough for the entire town to be concerned for his well being, so much so that they roused all of the people and mounted an all-out search for him late into the night. Still, this man felt that death was a better option than continuing to struggle in this life.

Unfortunately, suicide was a common occurrence in those times for these small towns. The most common mode was hanging, but people became resourceful and soon enough whatever got the job done was acceptable.

I will always be grateful to my parents, and my grandparents, for their resilience—instead of turning the cheek, and running away from their problems, they met them head on. They understood their capabilities as well as their limitations, and they persevered. Later, I learned that never once did my father mention, when he had to leave us, how unfair life was, and how difficult times had become. Instead, words of encouragement and support were lavished upon me.

Although part of a working community that valued hands in the fields instead of heads in the books, my grandparents and parents always supported me studying and gaining an education. I loved my little community, and I loved my family.

My life would be changed once again when I was four years old. At that time, my father had decided to call upon my mother and move her to help him in Venezuela with his newly formed business. He had found work as a shoemaker and seller with some partners, and it was time for him to start taking his family over, one by one. Unfortunately, I was not included in the request, and I was left to be raised by my maternal grandparents in Spain. As a child one learns not to question the decisions of adults, but it still is painful to be separated from your parents, especially at such an early age.

Nevertheless, this is when my relationship with my grandfather was really fortified. I don't know if it was out of a sense of responsibility to my mother, or out of a sense of pride from him, but my grandfather really loved and cared for me. As I said before, no matter what happened or what was said I could do no wrong in that man's eyes. If I said that the sky was green, by God that man would argue to the death that the sky was green. No matter what the situation, he was always there for me. In most ways, I believe that while I was growing up my grandfather was my best friend. I could confide in him, as well as rely on him for anything that I needed, and for that I will be eternally grateful.

Celso Rodriguez was an uneducated man, born and raised in Sabuz. He was small in stature, but immense in heart and attitude. He was a spitfire who didn't take any garbage from anyone, including his own family.

I remember one time, when I was young my parents sent enough money back to Spain in order to buy the small house in the town in which we lived. Before my family officially owned the house, I remember a cousin and I went to the house to cook a welcoming dinner, although the house still didn't technically belong to my parents. These were just minor trivialities in our mind. So, we continued anyway with our plan to cook our feast. As we put a pot on the stove and tried to heat up the contents, we may have been a tad careless with the amount of heat we were generating.

Needless to say, a small flame erupted from below the pot. We did what any two responsible children would do—we got out of there as fast as we could without telling anyone that there was a minor fire spreading inside the house. Luckily the vigilant owner was keeping an eye on the home, and he noticed smoke coming from it. He also noticed two small children sprinting for their lives out of the house.

I assume the gentleman extinguished the flames inside the house, but that only temporarily alleviated the flames in his head. He stormed over to my grandfather's house and screamed for him to come out. When he did, I could remember the man yelling, "Your granddaughter almost just set fire to the house." All that could run through my head was, "Oh man am I in trouble now." Instead, a reaction came that I can safely say would only come out of my grandfather's mouth. He calmly exited the house and screamed at the top of his lungs back towards the gentleman, "So what? It's their house. If she wants to burn it down who cares." Not exactly the typical reaction that you would expect from a man in his 50s regarding his six-year-old granddaughter, but, like I told you before, I could do no wrong in his eyes.

This credibility with my grandfather worked both ways. Although it gave me basically free reign to do and say what I pleased, it also gave me a long enough rope to hang myself figuratively.

As a child, I was what one would call a troublemaker. Actually, I considered myself so smart that I may have been a little bit of a bully. You have to remember there was no television, and we didn't have access to libraries or any great literature, so we were basically charged as kids to entertain ourselves. That's exactly what I did. In school, I would put thumbtacks in kids' seats, and put notes on their backs. Nothing too mean spirited was perpetrated, but enough to where, in hindsight, I can chuckle, but feel a little bad about it. As I mentioned, we had to entertain ourselves!

One great example of my antics was when my cousin and I were in the field near our family's livestock, and I decided to play a little trick on him. We had been asked to bring home some milk, and we obliged. On the way out, I made a deal with my cousin. I told him that in order to cut the time for the task in half, I would milk the cow, as long as he milked the horse.

Well, as we all know, it's never a good idea to milk a horse, especially a male horse. So, as I began to relieve the dairy cow of her milk, I kept a keen eye on the horse that my poor knucklehead cousin was now examining for the best way to extract the milk. Finally my cousin formulated his plan of attack. He made his approach and went in on the offensive. As he grappled with the horse, the animal immediately reacted and, nano-seconds later, the next thing we knew, my cousin was lying face up in the pasture staring at the clouds. After feeling the foreign hands on its underbelly, the horse reacted swiftly and applied a hoof directly into my cousin's chest. Upon seeing this, I erupted in laughter, pointing and teasing my poor cousin's misfortune. Hey, as I've already admitted, I was a little bit of a bully.

My inflated ego didn't always work to my benefit. Actually, at times it downright worked to my detriment.

My grandparents used to have a donkey that would pull the plow in the fields so that the crops could be sown. On this particular day, I had accompanied my grandfather to work in the field. As he was planting the crops and working on the soil, he called to me as I was playing. "Luisa," he said. "Go get the donkey so we can till the field." "OK," I said. As I was walking up towards the house where the donkey was kept, I could here him say, "Don't ride the donkey, because you're going to get hurt."

Well, in my arrogant mind, I didn't see this as a warning – I saw it as a challenge. I made my way up the hill and towards the house, where the donkey was tied up. Once I arrived, I untied the donkey, and instinctively disobeyed authority and mounted the steed. Unfortunately things didn't go as I had planned. A few gallops into my journey back to the field, the donkey did exactly as my grandfather had said it would, and he bucked me off. As I crashed down onto the hard cobblestone ground like a lifeless fish, I tried to break my fall and, in the process, successfully dislocated my elbow. On the ground, my first instinct was to cry like any other small child, but if I did my grandfather would come up the hill and realize that I had disobeyed him and had ridden the donkey. So, I composed myself, got up and tried to grab the donkey's rope to lead him down the hill. A shot of pain ran up my arm as I reached for the rope, and I realized that this might be a little more serious than I thought. No matter, I still couldn't let my grandfather know, or else I'd be in more trouble.

I walked slowly and gingerly down the hill, leading the donkey by the rope, and holding my injured arm, as still and in the most comfortable position as possible. I arrived down the hill, red faced and as rigid as a board. My grandfather could see right through me. Luckily, he was so concerned about the injury that he forgot about how mad he should be at me for not listening, and I didn't remind him. He took me to the doctor where they put me in a splint and all was forgiven, as my grandparents fed me chocolate and candy to take my mind off the pain. Still, I was a little too arrogant, and aloof; but, as they say, what goes around comes around. Karma has a way of catching up with us, and I guess this was my just desserts for tricking my cousin into milking a horse.

The way my grandfather reacted to this incident was indicative of our relationship. As long as he could make me smile, he knew that I was OK. Therefore, he did everything in his power to make me smile. He would take me to Bande, the nearest larger town, so that I could attend church. While in town, he would go to the café, drink his Schweppes club soda and buy me a hot chocolate. We would sit in the cafe talking and people-watching.

There was no television in our town, so whenever an important soccer match was on, my grandfather would ask me if I would accompany him to the bar to watch it. I didn't care about the soccer, but I got to spend more time with my grandpa, so I would always go, plus he would buy me more chocolate and candy. Our relationship was fantastic. He was the only father figure I had ever had in my life up to this point, and he treated me as though I were his daughter.

As they say though, all good things must come to an end. When I was seven years old, my father sent my mother to Spain to come get me and take me over to Venezuela to begin my new life with my parents. This affected me deeply. Although a child still, I had grown extremely emotionally attached to my grandparents. My mother arrived and stayed for a few days. The adults tried to make the transition as seamless as possible, but, on the day that we were to leave, I knew that things were about to change, and they would never be the same again.

The morning that my mother and I were to begin our journey to Venezuela, a taxi arrived to take my mother, my grandfather and me to the port where we were to catch our ship to our new home. As we were getting ready to leave, I went inside to say goodbye. The first person I saw was my uncle Emilio and his wife Maruja. I went over to them, my uncle wearing his trademark smile, which never left his face, and I said my goodbyes. I then set out to find my grandmother.

My grandmother was a very tiny lady. She had lived her entire life in small towns and rarely left the confines of these places. She never learned how to read or write, and she could not even speak Spanish. The only language she knew was Gallego, which is a dialect spoken in the region of Spain known as Galicia. She would only venture out of the town with an escort, and more times than not that escort was me. She was a quiet lady, but she was an incredibly loving woman.

As I went to say goodbye to her in the kitchen, her back was to me. I could tell she was either crying or had been crying, and in a soft voice she told me to go. She couldn't stand to say goodbye, the emotion of the moment was too much for her, and so I did as she wished. I turned around and left the house without ever saying goodbye to her. That was it, and in a blink I was gone. This was the only home I had ever known, and she was the main female figure in my life.

Looking back, I wish things had been different. I wish I had gone to her and hugged her. I wish that I had told her how much I appreciated all of her efforts in raising and caring for me. I wish that I had at least gone over and touched her or kissed her, or shown some sort of emotion as I was leaving, but to a child these things don't come to mind. I was leaving on another adventure with my mother, grandfather and this little taxi man. So, I turned and walked out of the only home I had ever known, got in the taxi, and left my town for a destination that was still unknown to me.

In the taxi, I could tell the mood was somewhat somber, but nobody put on any pretenses that this was a sad occasion. In my little mind, I guess I never thought that this would be the last time I would see Spain through the eyes of a child. The towns passed by, and the people worked and toiled in the fields as we sped through. To where? I didn't know.

Finally, the taxi came to a port town on the west coast of Spain. There were boats littered about the port. People were boarding and exiting massive ships. The taxi stopped in a designated area, and we made our exit. My grandfather helped the taxi driver with the luggage, and my mother went to make sure that everything was set with tickets and boarding for the trip back to Venezuela. I stood around taking in the sights. There were huge ships surrounding me, and the sound of the port was deafening.

People moved about, hustling merchandise on and off the cargo holds. The staff shuttled passengers aboard, while the crew tried to make sure that all the luggage and necessities were taken to where they needed to be. The merchants on the pier were also in their element. They hawked their wares to anyone who showed the remotest sign of interest in whatever it was they had to offer.

As we had time to spare, my grandfather said he was going to a nearby cafe so he could enjoy one of his favorite Schweppes. I helped the taxi driver get the luggage to where it needed to go, and then lost myself in my surroundings, enjoying the sounds of the pier. Before long, my mother returned with tickets in hand. She said that she had to go take care of something, and I was to remain with the taxi driver until she returned. I did as I was told and waited. I waited for what seemed an eternity with this strange man on this strange pier, feeling a bit uneasy.

Finally, my mother returned from wherever it was she had gone and took me by the hand. She looked at me and told me that it was time to leave and gather whatever things I had with me so we could board the ship. I did as I was told. As we were approaching the ship, I stopped short. I asked my mother where my grandfather was, and she looked down, and only told me that we had to go. I resisted. I told her that I wanted to see my grandfather before we left, and I was not going to get on that ship until I saw him. She tried to explain to me that it was too difficult, and we were running out of time. I resisted even more, and, by this time, I was growing a bit irritated at the insinuation that I would not be able to properly say goodbye to the only father I had ever known.

My mother motioned to the taxi driver who saw my growing agitation. She asked him to help her get me on board the ship; he scooped me up in his arms, with me crying and whining, and rushed me towards the passengers' embarkation. They got me to the ship and aboard without further incident.

I never saw my grandfather again that day prior to leaving for Venezuela. I never got the opportunity to give him a hug and tell him how much I loved him. I never had the chance to rap my arms around him and tell him how much I appreciated everything he had ever done for me, and I never got to tell him how much I enjoyed being his granddaughter.

The next time I would see my grandparents would be upon my return to Spain for medical school at the age of 16. Again, they would prove to be my biggest supporters and my biggest allies.

Some time later, I asked my mother why she did not let me say goodbye to my grandfather that day on the pier. Her only response to me was, "It was just easier that way." Easier for who – I don't know. You see, when she left me with the taxi driver, she had gone herself to say goodbye to my grandfather. She had told him that we were leaving, and she informed him that he would not have the chance to say goodbye to me. This affected him deeply. How do I know this? I know because, my mother told me the last sight she had of him that day as she was walking away was of him crying like an infant in the street and hugging a lamp post.

This man had more love in his heart for me than I could have ever imagined, and for this I must be eternally grateful. I hope that he knew that I had the same love in my heart for him.

CHAPTER 2

> "In the confrontation between the stream
> and the rock, the stream always wins,
> not through strength, but by perseverance."
> —H. JACKSON BROWN

The voyage from Spain to Venezuela took 13 days. The initial shock of not being able to properly say goodbye to my grandparents eventually wore off. I began to explore and discover new friends and places aboard this massive ocean liner. Our nights would be spent eating dinners with captain and crew. Afterwards, there was entertainment for all on board.

Maybe this is where my still-persisting love of cruises comes from.

The accommodations on ships in those days were significantly different from the accommodations on today's luxury liners. For starters, we did not have our own cabins/state rooms. Instead, people shared common living areas. There were large rooms with beds set up for approximately 15 people per area. This made it a lot of fun for the kids, as we had free rein to cause any sort of havoc that we pleased. For the most part, the days on board were uneventful, we had good weather, and there weren't any sort of crazy out-of-the-ordinary events that took place on our trans-Atlantic voyage.

We arrived in Venezuela in December, 1962. I can remember it as if it were yesterday. It was nighttime as the ship made its initial approach to the port city of Caracas. Caracas just happens to be the capital of Venezuela, and like all other capitals it had, and still has, its share of problems. On this night though, nobody could convince me of anything other than that this was the most beautiful place that I had ever seen. As the ship approached land in the distance we could see flickering lights. At first it began as a spot in the distance. As time passed and we neared the shore, the spot grew larger into a hazy blaze of illumination. Still, as the boat approached even closer, the different colors began to emerge. You could see yellow, red and green. Even closer now, the brilliant blues and oranges emerged from the background. Finally, we were close enough to land that we could make out the shape of houses and faintly see the activity of the people.

It was Christmas time, and what I was seeing were the ornamental lights that the people had strung up along their homes in the small shantytowns near the port. Although these ghettos are a sad reminder of the unstable and unfair economic conditions that people are sometimes forced to live in, on this night I told myself, as well as anyone who would listen, that I had never seen anything so beautiful in my life. There I stood on the deck of this massive ship, soaking in the luminescent bulbs from all sides. I had never been exposed to something like that, and I marveled at the sight of all of the beautiful colors.

I leaned my head against the rail of the ship, and became overcome with emotion. My mother looked at me and asked me what was wrong. My only response to her was that nothing was wrong. Indeed, nothing was wrong at all. My emotion was of pure joy, not sadness. You see, the lights and the houses to me were an ideal representation of a Christmas nativity. This scene onboard this ship, which was taking me to a new life in a strange place, had filled me with a renewed comfort, almost as if it were a sign from above assuring me that everything was going to be OK. I stood there on the deck of the ship, until it was moored at the pier, admiring all of the pretty lights that were a sign from above, as well as a large comfort to an otherwise scared little girl.

When I told my mother that I thought the ghettos were beautiful, she chuckled at my youthful innocence, and her only response to me was, "If you like this, you're going to love the rest." Although she was right in some respects, the homes in the ghetto in daytime were worn and dilapidated. But, this initial impression will always be the way I remember Venezuela, pure, warm, and welcoming to a little girl from a small farming village.

After retrieving our luggage from our living quarters, we made our way off the ship and onto the pier outside. People say they get butterflies in their stomach when they get nervous, well my stomach felt as though an elephant was being chased by a mouse in it. I was nervous for two reasons. First, the obvious, I was a stranger in a new country and had never been exposed to a city as big as Caracas. The size, at first, was quite overwhelming. That was not the major reason for my jitters, though. The second and main reason for my anxiety was the fact that when I got off the boat and onto the pier, there would be a man waiting there for my mother and me. This was a man that, as far as I remembered, I had never met, but had grown to love through stories, letters, and pictures shared with me through my family. Upon my exit of this ocean liner, my father would be waiting for me, and I would meet him for what, in effect, was the first time. If you remember, he had left Spain when I was two months old.

It was a very difficult concept for me to grasp – meeting my father now at the age of seven on a dark pier, after taking a 13-day cruise across a massive ocean, and away from the only home I had ever known. But that was exactly what was about to happen.

As we emerged from the ship, my mother grabbed my hand and led me towards the dock, where all of the family members were waiting. As we finally got to the throng of onlookers, my mother moved swiftly and with purpose. She dodged her way through people, cargo, and luggage, as if she already knew where her destination was. Apparently she did because, as we came to a clearing through the bustling bodies, there he was waiting with arms wide open.

I didn't know what to say, and I didn't know how to react, but instinct just kicked in, and I ran to him and jumped in his arms. He scooped me up off the ground and gave me a big hug and kiss. He held me in his arms for what seemed an eternity and all of the fear and anxiety that I was feeling not more than five minutes earlier disappeared in a flash. It seemed as though merely at the sight of him, I knew that this was my father and that even though this was my first time meeting him as far as I was concerned, I already had developed a bond with him, and I loved him. We shared our first moment as father and daughter on that pier that night in December 1962.

It had been a long time coming, but finally God had brought the three of us together again, and we were a family. Whatever hardships we would face, we would face them together as a family. I could see in my father's eyes that his perseverance had paid off, and he had finally reached one of the main goals he had set for himself. He had reunited his family, and he could now provide for us what he could not in Spain, a future, no matter how difficult attaining that goal would be for him.

Soon enough I settled into my life in Venezuela, and I adapted to my new surroundings. My family enrolled me into an elementary school near our house, and my parents worked their newly found trade of shoemaking.

At first, my parents worked as sort of a middleman for the factories and the market. Their job was to make sure that the merchandise got from the factory to the floor in a suitable time frame. As their knowledge of the industry grew, they began to take on higher responsibilities. Eventually, my parents were able to take on a partner and buy their own shoemaking factory. I can remember sitting around with my mother and their partner's two sons, making the cutouts for the shoes and also making advertising material for their company.

My parents worked long, hard hours. They would be up before dawn and would not return home until after the sun had set. The hours were arduous. They would occasionally work seven days a week, but they assuredly would never work less than six. It was a difficult transition for me, as I was accustomed to small town life with my grandparents being always easily accessible. This was not an option in Venezuela, though. In order to feed me and continue to help pay for my education, my parents had to work, and work they did.

While my parents were working long days, and I had a lot of time to myself, I continued on with my troublemaking ways. Upon arrival in the country, my parents enrolled me at the Escuala Divino Maetsre in Caracas, Venezuela. Although a great place, which offered great education, this was a Catholic School run by nuns. When they met me, the nuns thought I was the greatest thing since sliced bread. I was a good student who seemed to pay attention and not get into trouble, but I definitely took advantage of my most-favored-student status with the nuns.

For instance on a few occasions, when the nuns would leave the room unattended for a brief moment, they would undoubtedly ask me to be in charge of the classroom. I would always agree and, with a smile, jump at the opportunity to tackle this responsibility. After all, I was the girl from Spain who was the example in their eyes. When they would leave, they would give me some chalk and instruct the class that I had the authority to write the name of anyone who misbehaved on the board, which would lead to further sanctions. It doesn't bode well for the student body when one of the biggest troublemakers is also in charge of keeping order. It's a bit like letting the inmates run the asylum. Be that as it may, I would take full advantage of these opportunities. As a side note, looking back I really do feel bad about some of my childhood exploits, but we can't change the past now can we.

So, at times when left to my own devices, I indulged in the power bestowed upon me. I would order the kids to do things, and if they didn't do as I asked I would write their names on the board without reason. More often than not I would ask for favors, or lunch money, or even their lunch itself. If they obliged they were at a safe haven, but if they didn't listen, well then, they were in for some extra time with the nuns. No matter how bad I was, the nuns always believed me, and they continued to charge me with overseeing the room while they went elsewhere. Come to think of it, that was a lucrative time for an elementary school-age child.

My ability to take advantage of situations with the nuns made me more brazen in my follow-up attempts. After a while, they got very comfortable with me and learned to trust me with more and more responsibilities. The school would hold fundraising events, or money would be collected for field trips, and I would be designated the de facto treasurer for these gatherings. On certain occasions, which were few and far between, at the end of the night when it was time to collect the money, the nuns would come and ask me for a count and the cash. Every once in a while, I would take a handler's fee out of the profits without asking permission, and not report it to the nuns. When they realized that some of the funds were missing, they naturally would come to me and ask about what had happened to the money.

Imagine these grown women coming to a child in order to ask about missing money – unbelievable. Instead of coming up with some sort of clever response, or any reason as to why the money was gone, all I did was bat my eyes, and throw up my hands to say that's all that I had. Somehow this excuse worked every time. I don't know if it really worked or if it was that the money that I took was such a negligible amount that nuns were not overly concerned about my future as a thief. It could also have been that they saw right through me and noticed that my days of criminal enterprising were numbered, due to the fact that I was such a terrible liar. Be that as it may, they loved me, and I felt a sense of responsibility to validate that love through my studies.

I was always a good student, and during my time in Venezuela I was what many would consider a loner. The latter fact was more due to circumstance rather than choice. My parents working six to seven days a week from dawn till dusk forced me to spend a lot of time by myself. I relished in that alone time. It gave me a lot of freedoms at a young age that one would not normally assume a child to have, but it also forced me to mature rather quickly. I can remember times where my parents would be gone to work before I was up for school. I would have to feed myself breakfast and get myself ready for the day to come. I would then summon a taxi and go off to class by myself. After a full day of school, I would hail a taxi again and make my way home.

This regimen was repeated countless times over countless days, for a number of years. Through these experiences, I learned to rely on myself and God for most of my support, not to say that my parents were neglectful by any means, it was just the position we were in financially that forced us to spend most of our time apart. Whenever they could, they would try to make time for me. For instance, on weekends when they had some free time, we would pack a lunch and go to the beach to spend a day together. We also went to the movies, just the three of us, or for a family dinner to a local restaurant, but these ventures were few and far between due to the backbreaking hours that were required of them for work.

But provide for me they did. One thing I can say is that I was never without. If I needed something for school, or food, or clothes, my parents were always there to lend me a supportive hand. They also kept up with my schooling. In the big picture, it was important to them that I received a quality education, and, at the time, the best education was provided by the schools that had roots in Spain. So, when I became eligible for my secondary education, my parents made the decision to register me at El Instituto Espanol Cervantes. This institution provided what was the equivalent to our middle and high school education.

The school itself was registered and chartered in Spain, which gave it certain advantages over Venezuelan schools in my home country. Namely, I would not have to explain my curriculum if I decided to return home for any further education. This was the furthest thing from my mind at the time, but turned out to be utterly beneficial for my future endeavors.

I entered the school and began my journey to graduation. While on this journey, I made many discoveries about life, as well as myself. For instance, my position as a loner in life was solidified while attending my new school.

I have a memory so vivid in my mind of a ritual that I would perform, that it is hauntingly clear. I can remember doing my homework alone in my parents' house as a child, undoubtedly after the taxi man had brought me home. In the house, there was a great big bay window that overlooked the street in front of the house. I could see the activity of the city and the motion of the people on a continuous pace. I would typically ignore the hustle and bustle of the streets while doing my homework, but when it rained that all changed.

When I saw the storm clouds approaching, I would take a seat in front of the window and play some music in the background. I would wait for the clouds to approach and watch the impending storm form. When it finally arrived I would stay there in front of the window and cry as I watched the rainfall violently to the earth. I have no idea why I cried but I did, and, as I did, I would find a slight amount of comfort and solace in the fact that I was alone here in my home.

Rainstorms in Venezuela are a regular occurrence, and watching these storms form by that window also became a regular occurrence for me. To say that I enjoyed the sadness that filled my heart would be a lie, but to say that I did not appreciate the solitude that I enjoyed when by myself in those times would also be a departure from the truth.

Along with the revelation of my loner status during my time in Venezuela as a child, this was also the period when I began to become more cognizant of myself and my health.

Ever since I was a small child, I had been known to suffer from nightmares. They would occur regularly and, at times, would be so frightening that I would need family to wake me up from them due to my loud suffering.

The worst nightmare was the one that would consistently recur. It is as vivid in my mind today as it was when I was a child. I would be in a dark room, alone. It would smell damp and feel claustrophobic. Suddenly, I would try to move, and I couldn't; not because I was paralyzed, but because I was surrounded on all sides by closed-in walls. Then I would notice that I was lying down, and somehow a dim light would shine, and I could briefly see my surroundings. I was trapped in a coffin, and I was being buried alive. I couldn't scream, I couldn't pound on the lid, and nobody could hear me. In reality, I would scream so loud in my sleep that somebody would come and wake me. Later on, I was diagnosed as having night terrors, but, at the time, my family did not realize that this was an actual condition.

When I was still living in Spain I can remember having these dreams at my grandparents' small village home. In that house we only had one bedroom, which I shared with my grandparents. I had a smaller bed in the corner of the room, while they shared a larger bed across from me. When they heard me scream, my grandfather, God bless his soul, would take a shoe and throw it at me to wake me up from my sleep. He didn't know any better and, looking back on it today, his actions only serve to make me smile and miss his innocence.

While in Venezuela, my sleep conditions grew more complex. I developed the strange habit of sleep walking, as well as suffering from the night terrors. In one of the apartments that I shared with my parents as a child in Venezuela, we lived on the ninth floor of a Caracas high rise. My mother, the following morning, would retell me stories of my nighttime ventures throughout the apartment, of which I would have no recollection. She used to tell me that in the middle of the night I would walk into my parents' bedroom and sit on the foot of the bed staring out of the bedroom window. I would have entire conversations with her over a broad range of topics. She would tell me that these conversations would range in duration, and I would appear lucid during them. Once we were finished, I would walk back to my room and lay back down in my bed until the following morning. At breakfast, she would recount the events of the previous evening, and I would have absolutely no recollection of any part of our conversations, let alone walking to their room and sitting on their bed.

In comparison to what was to come, my sleep issues were the least of my health issues. Around this time, somewhere in the age range of 12 to 13, I began to experience the aches and pains that would eventually become a permanent part of my life.

I could remember waking up on rare occasions with aches in my joints ever since I was a small child, but around this time the aches and pains began to occur more frequently and started becoming more severe and prolonged. Until this time, I ignored them and just attributed the problem to stiffness and soreness associated with growth or normal childhood activity. Although young, I knew that this was not normal and something was wrong with me.

I feared the worst. I had no exposure to any sort of medical training, or anyone in my life with any form of formal medical training. I had heard stories of people waking up with these sorts of symptoms, and it scared me. Those symptoms included aches and stiffness all over my body. Generally, I would also be lethargic throughout the day, and my energy levels would be diminished through the least bit of physical activity. It was not just relegated to the morning time, either. At school, I always wanted to partake in the physical activities that all of the other children played in. I wanted to play soccer and tag with all of the other kids, but physically I was unable. I lacked the stamina and would become winded almost instantaneously. After a few minutes of exertion, I would be out of breath and gasping for air.

I had heard that these symptoms could be attributable to certain diseases, and I convinced myself that I was suffering from the worst of them. I thought that I was suffering from Leukemia, but where this idea came from I could not tell you even if I tried. This self-diagnosis was simply something divined from a child's imagination and a lack of information. Time only served to make me more certain of this diagnosis. Instead of getting better, the symptoms persisted. My energy levels decreased, my lethargy increased, and I became more limited in my ability to perform more exhaustive undertakings. To say that I was afraid would be an understatement. I was actually petrified, and alone. In some crazy way, I felt that this might be a sort of punishment that I was receiving for some unknown deed. No matter how scared I was, I refused to speak to anyone about my condition. The only person I spoke with was God.

I always had a close relationship with God, but now I began to pray to God with a purpose. I even went so far as to try to strike deals with him in exchange for my life. I would sit up at night and have conversations with him as if he was in the room with me. All these years later, I can vividly remember some of our conversations to this day. I would tell him that the only thing I wanted was to live until I was 20 years old. Twenty seemed so far away for such a young child, but to me it didn't seem like too demanding of a request. On a side note, once I got close to 20 years old, I started bargaining for 40 with the good Lord. I would sit up and speak to him, never angry, but always inquisitive. I began to question myself and search inside to find answers as to why this was happening to me. After many nights of inner seeking and soul searching, I came to the realization that this was my condition, whatever it may have been, and not a punishment, but rather a challenge that had been presented to me.

I realized then that God was not spiteful, only he had placed a roadblock before me, and he wanted to see how I would react. Would I fold and feel pity for myself, or would I rise and meet the challenge presented?

I decided I would take the latter road and try to attack the challenge head on. I never spoke to my parents about my symptoms; they never knew what sort of pain I was suffering from internally. As a matter of fact, the only health-related issue that they were aware I suffered from was anemia. The medical staff that diagnosed me as anemic attributed my sluggish nature and my inability to perform high-intensity tasks to this condition.

Little did they know that my anemia was a symptom of a much larger condition and not the underlying one. Be that as it may, I began to do my own research into my condition, and I decided that there was nobody on the planet that could help me other than myself.

This realization led to the natural conclusion that, in order to cure, or help myself, I would need to get some sort of healthcare training. Therefore, I would become a healthcare professional.

Most people when asked why they became a doctor would say something to the effect of, "I always wanted to help people," or list compassion for others as their main objective. Not me. The reason I decided to attend medical school and pursue a medical education was pure and simple. I wanted to cure myself of whatever it was inside that was causing so much pain. With that being said, I had no idea where to begin with my search for my cure.

Initially, I had thought that pursuing pharmacy would be my best course of action. There were pharmacy schools in Venezuela, plus if I knew what medications worked best for my symptoms I would be able to self medicate. This form of thinking, as I would come to find out, was flawed. I would still need the advice of a doctor, as well as one to prescribe me the medication. Also, I would not learn enough about underlying care to know exactly what it was ailing me. The last consideration was the state of the country itself.

Around this time, Venezuela began to fall into a pattern of crime and vice. All around, violent crime was on the rise, and drugs were beginning to become a real concern for the country's population. A lot of the country's youth began to turn away from education and towards the lure of easy money, the streets and a life of illicit gain. My parents noticed this trend in the youth, and, by this time, they had more to worry about than just me.

When I was 13 years old, my only sibling was born. I had a sister, and, to be honest with everyone, I was not too thrilled about it. It may sound selfish, but I felt as though I was too old to have a sister. And soon enough I was going to graduate from school, and I would more than likely be moving out of the house. So not only was my entire family dynamic as the only child about to be turned on its head, I also would not be around to really get to know my sister. I was used to being the only child, and, even though my parents were not ever able to lavish me with an exorbitant amount of attention, I did appreciate all of the attention that they were able to give me. I did not want to split this attention with anyone else, especially the amount that would be necessary for a newborn baby.

This led to the conversation that my family and I had to have in order to decide my future. There were a few options on the table. Devolution into crime was a symptom of a much larger plague that was ailing the country. Political instability was also on the minds of the population. This instability was affecting the educational system of the nation, as well as the country's morale. Therefore, my options were clear but they were difficult choices to be presented to a girl of 16 years. The conversation was brief, but poignant. I could either stay in Venezuela and pursue my medical education in that country, without knowing if my school would be shut down due to national crisis, as well as not knowing if the country itself would be thrust into anarchy pursuant to the rampant crime that was transpiring and increasing daily, or I could go back to Spain.

Spain was an option for obvious reasons; first and foremost, almost all of my family was there, so I had a built-in support system there. Second, I was familiar with the country, and I was comfortable in my surroundings there. Last, and most important of all, I was eligible to attend school in Spain because I graduated from a school in Venezuela that was registered in Spain, so I did not need to pass any further qualifying exams. I had the same rights and privileges as any student who had graduated from a Spanish secondary school.

My father balked at the idea of me going overseas. He felt that he had already missed out on enough of my life when he had to leave us to find work, and he did not want to have to go through a similar dilemma again. He gave every excuse as to why I should pursue my education in Venezuela and stay near my parents, but, in the end, reason and my mother's convincing prevailed. With that, the decision was made. I would return to Spain and say goodbye to my parents after only nine years of living with them in Venezuela. Those nine years would be the only years of my life that I lived with my mother and father for an extended period of time.

Soon after graduation, my father reluctantly made the arrangements for my travel back to Spain, my grandparents were alerted as to my return, and I packed my things preparing for my homecoming of sorts. This time, I did not make the transatlantic voyage by ship. I took a plane over, with no money and one small suitcase packed with my every belonging.

My parents had given me my directions for when I arrived in Spain, with the arrangements they had made with a cousin to pick me up from the airport and then take me to a train station. I said goodbye to them and began my journey on my naive quest to cure myself. On the flight over, I met this older gentleman with whom I struck up a conversation. After speaking to him and informing him that I had no money for when I arrived, he emptied his pocket of the change he was carrying and told me that I needed it a lot more than he did. I did not know it at the time, but, as luck would have it, he was more right than either one of us could ever guess.

CHAPTER 3

"We crucify ourselves between two thieves;
regret for yesterday and fear of tomorrow."
—*FULTON OURSLER*

To say that I was afraid of returning to Spain alone would be an understatement. I was only 16 years old and had nothing but a suitcase full of clothes, no money, and no idea exactly what future lay ahead of me. If I thought the idea of going back was frightening, I was definitely not prepared for what happened to me when I first landed back in Spain.

On the plane ride over, as I previously said, I struck up a conversation with an older gentleman who was returning to Spain from business overseas. He was a nice man with salt and pepper hair on top. He wore intellectual spectacles and spoke with an aura of academia. On the ride over, I told him of my plan to return to Spain and attend medical school. We got into a deep conversation about academics and life in Europe, in general. He was very knowledgeable, as well as very understanding. At the end of our conversation, he wished me well, and he reached into his tweed pockets and pulled out the loose change he had left. He looked at me and said, "I want to give you the first actual Spanish cash you will have." I said, "thank you," and I accepted his offer. Little did I know that his polite offering would come in handy much quicker than I could have ever imagined.

When the plane landed in Madrid, I was under the impression that my grandfather would be at the airport waiting for me to take me home. I was utterly mistaken, and what happened next would serve to be a lesson in life that I would never forget. I landed with a pocket full of change and a hunger for knowledge. When I exited the plane, reality not only hit me, but it smacked me across the face like a sack of two-ton bricks.

My parents had made arrangements for me to be picked up at the airport by a distant cousin, who I had not seen since I left Spain as a seven-year-old child. After retrieving me, this cousin was supposed to drive me to the train station where I would take a train for several hours to Orense, from where, my grandfather would pick me up and take me to my grandparents' house. When I landed, I collected my luggage and continued on past the baggage claim and out towards where people were awaiting the arriving passengers. I looked around for any familiar faces. I saw none. I looked around for anybody holding a sign with my name on it. No signs were there. I searched and searched inside the terminal, "Excuse me, sir, have you seen anyone looking for Maria Luisa Ferro?" "No, ma'am," was the response I heard over and over again.

Outside the terminal I went. I looked up high and down low, I searched for anyone and everyone that I could possibly think of in Spain, but still nobody came forward. I spent the better part of four hours searching the airport terminals for any signs of a familiar face. I saw none. I was lost, abandoned, had no way of communicating with my grandfather and stuck in what now seemed to be a foreign land. I could have folded and given up, but something inside me spoke to me. What I heard I did not necessarily want to hear. The voice said, "If you cry, nobody will help you, only you can help yourself." So I began to think pro-actively. I remembered an uncle in Venezuela who had given me the name of some people he knew in Madrid who owned a hostel for travelers. I dug out those coins that the man had given me, and I called information to get the address of this hostel.

There it was, the first Spanish cash that I had received what seemed only moments ago, being fed into the phone in order to try to help me get out of this nightmare of a mess in which I now found myself. The operator was helpful and resourceful. She gave me the information that I needed, but now I found myself in an even stickier predicament: how was I going to get to the hostel without any cash? Armed with my newfound information, I was determined to make the taxi driver understand and "no" would not be an acceptable answer for transportation. After a period of time negotiating, I finally found a taxi driver who would take me to the hostel in exchange for a promise of payment upon delivery.

I got into the taxi, and off we went. Another sense of dread overwhelmed me now: how was I going to convince the proprietors to pay for my taxi, as well as allow me to communicate with my family to figure out this mess? Unfortunately, the ride was nowhere near as long as I though it would be. We arrived in what seemed to be mere seconds, and there I was without a plan. I had nothing, but I had to think fast. I got out of the taxi as the driver was unloading my luggage. He asked for his fare, and I told him I had to speak with my friends upstairs in order to procure the fare. What friends upstairs? This was the only thing that kept repeating itself inside my head over and over again.

The driver agreed, but he also said he would keep my luggage as collateral until I returned with his fare. "Great, now this guy's going to steal my clothes," I thought, "what else could happen to make this day any better?" So, I climbed the stairs on a mission that I considered impossible. I arrived at the top landing, without any idea of what I would say to the face on the other side of the door, where I, confidently and rhythmically, heard the sound of the proprietor. The door opened, "Hello," said the frail older lady who appeared from within. "Hello," I said in return. I explained to her my entire situation, as well as underscoring the urgency and need to borrow some money, as there was a man holding my luggage hostage at the base of her stairs. She was, as you can guess, extremely confused to begin with, but when I gave her my uncle's name and explained the unfortunate mishap at the airport, she was nothing but gracious.

The proprietor lent me the money to pay for the fare, and took me into her home as if I were not a stranger at all, but family. She allowed me to use the phone, from which I called my family to try to find out what exactly happened to my ride, and where my cousin was that was more important than picking me up at the airport. And she fed me and gave me a place to stay until my cousin could properly receive me.

The lesson of that day was a resounding one, and I will never forget it. It is a lesson that my husband and I have hopefully instilled in our children over the years, and, simply put, the lesson is as follows: Nobody in this world is going to do anything for you unless you ask, if you sit there wallowing in your sorrows you will sit there forever. If you take action and ask for help along the way, the worse thing someone can say is no, then you can just move on to the next, but they can never say yes unless you ask. It is a simple lesson, but a valuable one, nonetheless.

I finally got hold of my grandfather in Orense and asked him about my ride situation. It appeared my cousin was not the sharpest tool in the shed. You see, the last time I had seen him was right before I left for Venezuela, when I was seven years old. Nine years had passed, and I was now 16. This genius, though, still pictured me as a nine-year-old, and, when he did not see any little girls wandering the airport terminal, he left thinking that other arrangements had been made. Like I said, not the sharpest tool in the shed!

Regardless of that fact he was a nice guy, and he profusely apologized for his blunder. He came to the hostel to retrieve me and my things, after my grandfather had straightened him out, and immediately put me on a train to my grandparents house where my grandmother had told me she had a big surprise waiting for me. After all of this mess, the only big surprise I had hoped for was a room with a nice warm bed.

Once I arrived at my grandparents' house, I was reminded of exactly how small a town I really came from, and exactly what sorts of things passed as big surprises around these parts.

It turned out that there was no separate room with a warm bed and new sheets. No, my little grandmother, God bless her soul, had been hard at work preparing a meal for me as a big surprise. Looking back, I realize how special these people were indeed. She had sliced her best Chorizo, Spanish sausage, from her prized pig, and had marinated it in special oils for my arrival. What was special about the oils? I have no idea, but in this instance I did not care one bit. I just knew that everything that was done for me here was done out of complete love. A warm feeling came over me there in my grandparents' house. It was a feeling that had been missing for some time. It had been missing since I had left over nine years earlier, and the only way to describe the feeling that overwhelmed me there and then, with the Chorizo surprise before me, was that I was home.

I arrived in Spain in June 1972 to find things had changed. I was now a young woman and accustomed to a faster pace of life than when I was a child in Spain. Before beginning medical school, I had to enroll and complete pre-requisite classes that were to be taken at the medical college in Santiago de Compostella. These classes included basic sciences, as well as background mathematics that would be required later on in the medical curriculum. One problem was that these classes did not commence until September. So, here I was a sixteen-year-old in a small farming town with about 200 residents with literally nothing to do for the next three months. The days grew long and tiresome rather quickly, as you can imagine. When you are a teenager used to the fast pace of a capital city, such as Caracas, Venezuela, you can only take so much of cattle herding and crop tending before you start to become a little stir crazy and develop cabin fever.

So what did I do? Well, I did the only logical thing that I thought I could do. I looked for, and enrolled in, a program in Orense for typing.

Why typing, you may ask? Well, I really don't have a creative answer for that question, save for the fact that it was the only way to get out of the small town and keep myself occupied for the next three months until I moved to Santiago de Compostella to begin my medical education. So, off I went to learn how to become the world's greatest clerical assistant, or at least a proficient typist. I moved into what they referred to in Spain as a "pension."

A pension in this regard was a place where students lived and paid rent to the owners of the building. It was usually a place with only a few students, and they received their meals, as well as room and board and cleaning services in exchange for the monthly rent paid. It is similar to a sorority house here in the United States, except on a much smaller scale and without the organizational affiliation. I went to Orense for those three months basically to kill time. As expected during the week, I would attend class and complete my coursework, and on the weekends I would take a bus back to my grandparents' house in Sabuz to spend time with them.

The time there flew by. Although I can honestly say that I attended and attempted to learn the art of typing, I believe that it was a wasted effort on my part. You can ask anyone in my family, and they would tell you I am not the most graceful of creatures when it comes to maneuvering around a keyboard.

Be that as it may, the time had come for me to enroll in the prerequisite medical course at the University of Santiago de Compostella. I was filled with emotions: I was excited about beginning my career education, I was nervous about moving to a new city so far away from my family alone, and I was also a little bit scared about how I was going to be able to accomplish all of the things that I wanted to do so I could make my family proud.

Arrangements had been made for me to stay at the home of my grandmother's brother. He was married to a Catalonian lady with whom, from the beginning, I could sense tension. As soon as I arrived in the home, I began to experience weight gain, as well as stomach aches. At the time, I attributed these symptoms to the food she was making, but looking back on it they could have been due to the disease, which was beginning to manifest itself rapidly. To say one way or the other what brought on these symptoms would be speculation, but it really is inconsequential as I did not remain in the Catalonian woman's home for very long.

As I said before, we did not get along from the start, and she began making a little bit too much noise about me to too many people. We would get into arguments and heated discussions, and she would threaten me with punishments and evictions. Anyone who knows me understands that I do not take well to threats. It has always been that way, so when she began to threaten me, I began to resist any of her requests or demands, and our relationship further soured. One day, it finally came to a head, and she had the gall to call my father in Venezuela to demand that he come and pick me up from her house and take me back home. I laughed at her and told her I was not going anywhere. She didn't take that response too well. I was certain that I had done no wrong, and I was already tired of listening to her myriad of complaints about me. I told my father I was not leaving, but I also told him that I was not staying with these people anymore. You can imagine in what sort of situation this put my father across the Atlantic Ocean in Venezuela, having to deal with a stubborn daughter and a woman who was upset that I was not doing enough cleaning around the house to satisfy her. So, he did the only thing he could. He called my grandfather to deal with the situation.

My grandfather arrived in Santiago shortly thereafter. As you already know, I could do no wrong in that man's eyes, and anyone who dared speak ill of me would feel the full range of his wrath. As you can guess, this woman received the tongue lashing of her life. Once he arrived, he had me pack all of my things, and he took me out of that house quicker than the blink of an eye. All the while, he was swearing and yelling at this woman for having the audacity to even insinuate that his granddaughter could have caused any grief or created any hardship in her household.

In retrospect, maybe he was a little bit hard on her, but that's how my grandfather was. He was fiercely protective of me, and he would defend any decision or action that I took.

Now I was facing a completely different problem. School was still in session. I was a new student only starting my pre-requisite courses, I did not have many friends and the ones that I did have did not have their own houses. I was now, for all intents and purposes, a homeless medical student in Santiago. This was a byproduct of the meltdown with the Catalonian woman that I had not anticipated. So, at the age of 16 and in the middle of my first semester, I was stranded. My hero, my grandfather, had already accounted for this situation prior to coming to Santiago. He had called my godfather, who was familiar with the Santiago area, and asked him for a reference of a good pension for the time being. It was meant to be a band-aid or a quick fix until we could find something more permanent the following semester.

My godfather had given my grandfather the name of a lady who ran a pension in the city that he highly recommended. Her name was Senora Chucha and her husband, Senor Manolo. Armed with this reference, my grandfather grabbed me and took me directly to this pension. We arrived later in the afternoon and knocked on the door. Here I was still a child, all things considered, already evicted from my first house and frightened that my schooling could be in jeopardy. Senora Chucha opened the door, and my grandfather introduced himself and me to the lady of the house.

He went on to explain the situation that I was in, and the uncommon predicament that we, we being I, now found ourselves. He told her that she came highly recommended by my godfather, whom she knew, and that we needed a place for me to stay. Everything was going splendidly until she dropped the bomb. They were full. All of the rooms in the pension had been leased already, just like all the rooms in all of the surrounding pensions likely were. You see, these pensions, as I mentioned earlier, were the places where students lived all over the country. This particular pension had been filled since the beginning of the semester. She apologized to my grandfather profusely and told him how much she wished that she could help us, but she simply had no room.

Now I really began to get nervous. Anxiousness and my anger towards that damn Catalonian woman began to grow in my belly like a roaring fire. Senora Chucha went on to tell my grandfather of some neighboring pensions that might have some room and even went through the trouble of offering to help us find a room somewhere.

My grandfather declined. He explained to her what he believed she did not understand. He pulled her aside and said, "This is my only granddaughter, and you were the only people recommended to me. She is either staying here, or she is coming home with me." She insisted that she had no room, which was true as all of the rooms in the pension were occupied and had been so since the beginning of the semester. The more she insisted, the more my grandfather persisted that I stay there. He simply would not take no for an answer, and finally I think the lady of the house understood this fact. After what seemed a lifetime of friendly discussion and adoration poured upon her by my grandfather, she went to her husband to see what, if anything could be worked out.

That night, I moved into the pension where I would live for the next five years of my life. My grandfather convinced them to take me in, even though they had no vacancies available at the time. If there were no vacancies, where did I sleep? My grandfather was so persistent and convincing that he had somehow persuaded these wonderful and gracious people to allow me to sleep in their bedroom. Yes, you read that correctly. I was now not only living under their roof, I was sharing their bedroom, as well. They pulled in a cot that they had for unexpected guests, set it up in their room, and there I slept for the remainder of my pre-requisite year of medical school.

I think the reason that they allowed me to share their bedroom was a combination of many factors. After moving in, I felt as though these two wonderful people were not only allowing me to stay because of the monthly rent they were collecting, but rather they saw me as somewhat of a daughter to them. After all, I was only 16 years old, I was in a strange town, I didn't know anyone, and all I wanted to do was go to school. They saw something in me that day, and I hope that in the long run I was able to affirm that belief they had in me.

Classes were going great, and I was starting to get the hang of Santiago. I had a wonderful place to stay, with genuine people, and not a care in the world rather than studying. My routine was simple. I would get up early in the morning and have a prepared breakfast. I would shower, go to class, and study until night. When I returned, my area would be clean and my bed would be made. I had a meal waiting and no complaints about anything at all. After supper I would either study more, or possibly go out with friends to a local nightclub to dance. All was well with school, and Christmas time was upon us.

I was quickly finding that out that the weather in Spain was different from the weather in Venezuela. I guess the weather was never really a concern to me as a child, so I had blocked it out of my mind, but coming from a tropical location to a place where winter is about as brutal as it can get was a lesson quickly learned.

After exams, I went to my grandparents' house for Christmas break. I had made the journey to visit them many times throughout the semester, and each time it was an all-day affair.

In order to get to my grandparents house from school, I had to take a train from Santiago to Orense. Once in Orense I needed to take a taxi from the train station to the bus depot. From there, I had to take a bus from Orense to Bande. In Bande, my grandfather would always be waiting for me at the cafe drinking his coffee, and we would take a taxi together to their house. In order to make this trip you would have to allot at least a full day of travel because, even though the distance was not too significant, you must remember these were rural parts of the country where transportation ran on its own time.

So, off I went to spend my first Christmas as an adult in Spain with my grandparents. The holiday was wonderful, and the break from school provided a much-needed mental rest, especially considering all of the drama that took place in those first few months. While back, I tried to keep busy and help out around the house as much as I could. I did chores, such as cleaning dishes and counters. I would scrub floors and generally do anything that was asked or needed to be done.

It was during this time also that the first visible signs of my rheumatoid arthritis developed. One day, while scrubbing the floors in my grandparents' house, I noticed a lump on my left wrist. I was on my hands and knees using an old brush and scrubbing with incredible vigor. Ironically, I did not recall hitting anything or any trauma to that area, but I decided that I must have hit my wrist against something and this was just a bruise. Time went by and the lump on my wrist did not change. Some days it would be smaller, some days it would be larger, but it just would not go away. The lump would shift locations along my wrist to the back of my hand, but nonetheless it would never disappear. What I thought was a bruise at the time would never heal.

Thinking back, I now know the reason for the varying size and location of the lump along my wrist. This lump was a fluid-filled sack underneath the skin that was positioned along the wrist joint in my left hand. On the days that the fluid was reabsorbed into the bone – good days – the lump would be smaller and more retracted towards the joint, and on the days when the lump was more prominent and visible, the fluid would re-concentrate in the area of my wrist and the top of my hand.

At the time, I had no idea what this ailment could be. I still had not been to a primary care physician, let alone a specialist, to try and diagnose what this lump could possibly be signaling.

Time had come for me to return to school and leave my grandparents house for the remainder of my pre-requisite course year. The lump on my wrist was still present, and it was of growing concern to me. I did not know what it was, it was not sensitive to the touch, and it never changed color like a normal bruise would. By this time, I was resigned to the fact that it was definitely not a bruise, but it was something that I needed to be concerned about. I approached one of my professors, Dr. Dominguez, who was a noted genius in his chosen field, and was also a physiology professor at the school. I approached him shyly and presented him with my dilemma. I informed him of my name and who I was, telling him that I was a pre-requisite student at the university, and asked him if I might have a brief moment of his time. I recited the story of how the lump mysteriously appeared on my wrist one afternoon after performing some medium-intensity chores at my grandparents' house, and also informed him of the amount of time that had passed since that incident. I told him how I did not recall any trauma to the area, and basically told him all of my symptoms. This doctor, this professor, this world-renowned brain in his field, gave me probably one of the worst diagnoses ever to come from a medical professional. Instead of looking at the lump, or examining it, or even getting a basic medical history of me, this man looked me straight in the eye and basically dismissed me as a nuisance. This professor told me in order to cure the lump, and to rid myself of whatever was causing it, I should take my anatomy book, and put it on my wrist while I was studying so the lump could be pressed away by the weight of my book. Now I know everyone has been able to find better uses for study material than as actual study material, but let's be serious – this was a little beyond ridiculous.

I retreated to my studies, and attempted to concern myself with school. The lump never went away, but, stubbornly, I did not seek any real medical attention. The first year passed and I did well in my studies, so I was granted acceptance into the medical program of the university. Then, other symptoms began to manifest themselves. We had gone through one of the famous northern Spain cold winters, and the body reacts differently to the cold when it is used to a tropical atmosphere. One would expect to get shivers, and aches and pains from the weather, but mine seemed to be a little out of the ordinary. I began to experience weight gain, but I thought it was because the food I was eating might have been too rich in olive oil. I began to experience more serious bouts of lethargy, and it became increasingly difficult to maintain the energy levels necessary for the normal activities of my life. Finally, I began to experience what many people refer to as medical-school syndrome. Any topic that was covered, be it disease or virus, anything from West Nile to Ebola, I diagnosed myself as having that affliction. Things got worse the deeper we delved into illnesses, and I began to drive myself mad. I associated the lethargy, the weight gain, the joint pain and stiffness with every imaginable disease known to man.

By this time, I had already turned 18, I was in my second year of medical school and my mind was going mad trying to figure out exactly what was happening internally with my body. By this time the joint pains had become more severe, especially in my knees. The fluid would collect and the joints would be inflamed. My knees would sometimes swell to twice the size that they normally were. I tried to hide the symptoms by wearing long pants and covering my knees as much as I could.

Back at school, I had continued with multiple self diagnoses. One day it was lung cancer. The next day it was breast cancer. I had them all. There was no differentiation; whatever we would cover that day, or that week, I was able to associate all diseases with whatever it was that was causing my suffering. Make no mistake about it either, I was suffering. Normal activities began to become difficult. Getting out of bed in the morning had become a chore like none other. I had begun to incorporate more time in the mornings to allow for my joints to warm up, and the pains to run their course. Walking became an exercise that necessitated a sufficient grace period before becoming a normal everyday activity. Things were difficult, and they were only growing more and more difficult with no cure in sight.

Finally, one day in class the professor broached the subject of rheumatology. He began to describe the nature of the disease, as well as the symptoms from which those who have the disease typically suffer. The professor described the joint pain, the lethargy, the stiffness and aches, everything from which I was currently needlessly suffering. He even described the weight gain that I had been blaming on the cooking oil. This lecture hit home with me, and I decided to finally seek medical attention with a focus on rheumatological disease. I found a general physician who diagnosed me with rheumatoid arthritis.

At last, I had a sense of relief. All of those terrible disease, all of the cancers that I had condemned myself to or had, were not what was causing me all of my pain and strife. Now though, I was faced with a different reality. I knew what I was suffering from, but how could I treat it? The first doctor who diagnosed me generally addressed the fact that I suffered from some form of rheumatological disorder. He prescribed me prednisone for treatment, which is in a class of medications called corticosteroids. These drugs work by preventing the release of substances in the body that cause swelling and inflammation. Prednisone is an invasive drug, and the side effects of it are serious and can cause severe complications. The drug itself can weaken the user's immune system, which, in turn, makes it easier for the patient to be subjected to infection, or worsen an already existing infection.

There are physical external changes that occur while on such a medication, as well as internal changes. People on prednisone can experience unusual weight gain and personality changes, as well as puffiness of the face. Along those lines, people may also experience changes in the general shape of their body; for example, body fat may begin to concentrate in new areas, such as the arms, legs, face, and neck.

Although the side effects can be serious, the medication is a very effective treatment against the symptoms of RA. I did have some issues with the medication that I was wrongly attributing to outside environmental factors. For instance, I had been experiencing rapid weight gain since being on the medication, but I thought it was due to the oil in the foods that I was eating. My face had begun to take on a round almost soccer-ball shape, but I also attributed that to the food and the weight gain.

The medication helped, but I had begun to notice changes in my mood, as well as the physical changes in my body. I never did like going to see doctors, so naturally I did not want to set up an appointment just to complain about some mood swings and weight gain, especially since the medication was helping relieve some of my symptoms, and I now had an answer as to what was going on with me internally. I did not want to seem ungrateful, and really had no complaints with regard to the diagnosis. As a matter of fact, the only problem with me being on this medication and my initial visit with this man was that I was never told for how long I was supposed to take the prescription medication, nor was I told what effects it would have on my body.

After being on the medication for some time, I had started to experience more severe side effects. I had unexplainable bleeding; I also began to experience severe abdominal pain that would last for prolonged periods of time. After a while, I decided I could not live under those circumstances. I had traded one set of problems for an entirely different and new set of possibly more severe problems. I decided that maybe it was the prednisone reacting with my body that was making me have these abnormal changes. I decided to go off the medication for a while, and pulled myself off cold turkey one day. Boy was that ever a huge mistake on my part. You see, when you are on a medication, such as prednisone, you are basically giving your body a dose of something that it produces naturally. In the case of prednisone, you are supplementing substances produced in the adrenal cortex of your brain in pill form. After a while, your body gets used to receiving this dosage in pill form, and it stops producing it on its own. Because your body is receiving a sufficient amount from an outside source, your adrenal glands shut down on their own, stopping production of the supplemented hormone. Well, when you try to stop taking that outside source you must level off at a slow pace so as to allow your body to get back on track and start producing the hormone in the proper levels. As you can imagine, stopping cold turkey was not a smart choice on my behalf.

I did not feel the full effects of my decision for a few days after stopping my medication. I was at the house of my best friend in medical school, Mary Carmen, who was also a medical student. We were eating dinner with her parents having normal conversation. I had been feeling a little ill for some time throughout the day, but nothing of substance, and nothing that I thought needed immediate medical attention. The meal was served, and all was well. Mary Carmen was telling her parents about her day, and they, too, asked me about mine. It was pleasant and very familial. I remember I was reaching across the table for something, and then, all of the sudden, everything went blank. Things did not necessarily go blank, but things were "otherworldly."

I remember sitting in my chair, and then it felt like I was not there anymore. I was in the room, but I was not in my body. I felt as though I had been jolted out of my body, and I was now floating over myself looking down at all of us as if watching a scene in a movie. I was numb, I could not move, I was frozen in space. Everything was weightless including me, and I could not feel, touch or sense anything tangible. I could see my carcass sitting in that chair with a blank look on my face, but with no movement, no speech, and no recognition of my surroundings, when suddenly another jolt hit me, and I was flung back into my chair. When I came to, I was understandably confused. I was surrounded by Mary Carmen and her family, all asking if I was OK and what had happened. I sat there in my chair assessing my situation. I was out of breath, my heart was racing, and my mind was as clouded as the San Francisco fog. I could not find the words to describe what exactly had just taken place, because I myself was unsure of exactly what had just occurred. So, I told them that I was fine, and that I just was not feeling well. I could tell that they were skeptical of my response, but they were such kind people that they did not want to press me, especially after what they had just witnessed.

Later on, my friend told me that we were in conversation, and dinner had been pleasant with no signs of anything out of the ordinary. Suddenly I froze, and it appeared that I may have been suffering a stroke or a seizure, as my entire body tensed and the muscles of my face appeared to have been locked in a permanent stare. This lasted for a few moments; meanwhile her parents attempted to snap me out of whatever spell I was currently under. It was of no use. I could not be brought out of it. Finally, she said, I shook, and convulsed violently for a moment and snapped out of my haze.

You hear many people describe what they refer to as out of body experiences, and sometimes they sound resoundingly like dreams or hallucinations. I myself have been skeptical of people's accounts of these supernatural experiences where they claim they float above their bodies to witness their surroundings in a sort of third-party perspective. I mean, I was skeptical of them until that evening at dinner at Mary Carmen's house. All things accounted for, this episode was, I feel, strictly due to me stopping my prednisone medication without any warning or slow reduction of dosage. My body had not been producing the necessary hormones, and this was obviously a drastic side effect of that extreme depletion of outside hormone. I also took away from this experience some valuable lessons. The first was the seriousness of the medications that I would be dealing with for the rest of my life in regards to this disease.

The resounding lesson that I took from this experience was something far greater. As I have already described in previous chapters, I was what most would consider a loner growing up. Having to be shipped to my grandparents' house, then to my parents and then back to Spain, I never had any real sense of belonging to a family, in the traditional sense. There was something missing that I could not quite put my finger on.

When I began to spend time with Mary Carmen, and her family, I realized what that feeling of emptiness was. I was feeling a void of belonging. I had a sense that I needed to be accepted by people, but not just any person, a family. I had never thought in these terms before because I had never really known what it meant to belong to a stable family. But seeing the interactions of my friend and her parents, as well as the way they welcomed me into their household, made me sad and hopeful that one day I, too, could feel as though I belonged to something far greater than just myself. One day, I might have my own stable family.

I grew from this semi-religious experience at Mary Carmen's home, vowed to take better care of myself, and began researching medications and looking into a care regimen for controlling the symptoms of my disease. I had a friend by the name of Mary Belle who was a pharmacy student and worked in a laboratory as an intern. I would go there from time to time and ask the lab technicians to draw my blood so they could check on my iron and other levels to make sure everything was OK. I began to ask questions about medications and tried to figure out how and even if my RA would interact with my lifelong anemia. A natural follow up was how and if any medical regimen would affect these two distinctly different conditions.

It was a difficult time early in medical school, but I'm afraid that I am making it sound as if I was always cooped up in my room studying, or in some lab drawing blood from one of my veins like a mad scientist. This could not be any farther from the truth. I attended medical school and lived in Spain in a time of peace and tranquility. We were young adults who were responsible, but we were also young adults who knew how to have a good time, just like any other college-age students. Santiago de Compostella was like any other college town. We had our little cafes where I would meet friends in between classes. We also had our little bars where at night we could meet for tapas and a glass of wine. I vividly remember another close friend in particular Mary Carmen Cacheda, for the long lunches we would share at her family's home where we would indulge on Sundays in strawberries and left over wine that her uncle who was a priest would bring us. There were dance clubs where students would go to unwind, and dance the night and all of their troubles away. It was a great time to be a student and a great time to live in Spain. It was safe, I was surrounded by friends, and, up till then, I was learning to cope with my disease.

Then I hit a stumbling block along the way. After my prerequisite year, I gained entry into formal medical training. I dove into my studies that first semester of medical school, and took my studies as seriously as I could. But something was off. I did not seem to be grasping the material the way I thought I should be, and that reflected in my first semester grades. Of the four classes that I was enrolled in, I passed only one. I failed three. I could not progress in the program, and was left at an impasse. The news was devastating to me, as you can imagine. I had lost all interest in medicine and booked a flight back to Venezuela. I came home to my parents' house dejected and broken. More than anything, I was feeling pity for myself.

I sat down with my father and told him that I was not going to return to Spain, and I had no desire to pursue medicine as a career anymore. He spoke to me and reasoned with me, instead of becoming angry. He asked me if I felt defeated and afraid, or if I truly did not want to pursue medicine as a career. He told me that it was OK to fail, but what really matters is how someone reacts to that failure. Through his words, I came to understand that I did love medicine, but I was angry. I had failed, but I did not have to give up. He gave me an option, I could go back to Spain and give it another shot, or I could stay home. The choice was mine. He told me he could not make any decisions for me, but that he would support any decisions that I made. After our conversation the decision was simple – I would return to Spain and give it another shot.

And that is exactly what I did. In the spring, I returned to Spain and enrolled in the exact same curriculum that I had failed only a semester before, and this time I received not only passing but above-average marks in all four courses. After that speech with my father, I never doubted my motivation, or desire to become a physician again.

I fell back into my normal rhythm with my friends from school, striking that balance between fun and school. All the while, I still had not found a satisfactory regimen to control the symptoms of my RA. It had been progressively getting worse, and with the winter now upon Spain the mornings had become excruciating. I would wake up in the middle of the night, dreading the morning, because I knew that it would take a significant amount of pain and effort simply to get out of bed. Not only that, but in order to take a hot shower in our pension, I had to pay an increased rate for the hot water that I used. To ensure that there was hot water at the time was another matter completely. Just because I had a right to the hot water, did not mean there would be hot water available, especially in the dead of winter. Through it, I persisted, and I continued to press through the grind of school.

That grind was made easier by the friends that I had been blessed to find. They were all great, but two, in particular, I considered to be my best friends and my first true support system. First, Mary Carmen and her family gave me a sense of belonging by welcoming me into their home in Santiago with no questions asked. She was my study partner throughout school, and she was also my partner in crime, so to speak. We were inseparable and, at times, that could be dangerous. Literally dangerous, as evidenced at the time when we locked ourselves in her room to "study." We had an odd tradition prior to studying, which we indulged in not too infrequently. We would eat canned sardines and share a bottle of champagne between the two of us, then settle down for a night of intense studying. We had both already taken up the unhealthy habit of smoking, but in those days in Europe you could not find a soul our age who did not partake in the habit. Although now we know all the harmful, nasty side effects of smoking, these were not widely recognized in those days, and the power of advertising back then made smoking seem just so incredibly cool. Anyway back to my story, we were two teenage women, studying after a stuffing ourselves with canned fish and drinking an entire bottle of champagne, locked in a tight space smoking cigarettes with all the doors and windows closed to keep out the cold winter air. I'm sure most of you can see where this story leads, but I'll finish it anyway.

At some point in the night, after a few hours of studying and a few more cigarettes smoked, we both fell asleep in our books. Now that sounds innocent enough, except for the fact that Mary Carmen had thrown a cigarette in the trashcan without extinguishing the lit ember just before she fell asleep. Suddenly, an orange glow erupted in the trashcan as all of the papers inside caught ablaze, and the intense heat, as well as the smoldering smoke, poured from inside of the container. I woke up suddenly to the smell of the smoke, and the bright glow of the fiery trash and paper. I screamed and woke Mary Carmen up. We both sprang into action to put out the impending conflagration. With disaster averted, we sat down, laughed at the situation, assessed the damage, which was minimal, and did what any other two college students would do. We lit a cigarette to calm our nerves back down.

We were inseparable. We liked the same food, we liked the same wine, and we even liked the same music. We had a tradition of listening to Beatles records while we studied. We had no idea what they were saying in their songs because we did not speak English, but we knew we liked their music nonetheless. Mary Carmen and her family made me feel as though I fit in, and they never judged me, or made me feel any sort of embarrassment around them for my disease, and for that I will be eternally grateful to these wonderful people.

Another friend with whom I had a similar relationship was Mary Belle, the pharmacy student. Mary Belle was my roommate in the Senora Chucha's pension. We met there and quickly became friends. She was from a completely different background from me; her father was an Olympic champion and had won a medal for Spain in the Berlin Olympics. They enjoyed opera and traveling, and they lived a very comfortable life in A Coruna. Her father was extremely well read, intelligent and scholarly. Where I was rural, they were urban, but they never once made me feel as though they were superior to me in any way. Quite the opposite, they would invite me everywhere with them, they would teach me about travel, and they would welcome me into their home and along with them on their adventures. They had all the ability to be your typical upper-crust snobs, and they had the pedigree to do it, but they never once ever gave the impression of being above anyone else. In fact, they treated everyone with respect and dignity, and made me feel welcome from the moment I met them.

Mary Belle and I had a great friendship, as well. Being roommates, we had ample opportunity to become close friends and influence each other. She would drag me to her opera, and I would force her to come to the dance clubs. It was a great give-and-take relationship, which exposed me to many fun and exciting opportunities that I would have never experienced had I not met her and her influential family. Although our tastes were different in many ways, in certain respects they were eerily similar.

As a matter of fact, a great example of our similarities came to light when Jesus Christ Superstar the movie which had just been released was shown in the local cinema for a two-week stretch. We went to watch it together and liked it so much that, for the next two weeks straight, we went and watched the movie every day. No matter rain, sleet, snow, night or day, we were there watching Jesus Christ Superstar. It became such a tradition, that we began going to see the movie on the weekends in our pajamas. It was never forced on either of us, and it was never an issue, we went because we loved it. It was as though we were sisters, and her family treated me as such. On family vacations they asked me to go with them, daytime outings I was invited, parties always included an open offer to join them. They even took me to see my first live Tom Jones concert, on the Spanish leg of his tour. For their warmth and hospitality I will be eternally grateful to Mary Belle, as well as her family. Mary Belle and Mary Carmen's family were the first people to show me stability and acceptance. In no way do I mean that as an insult to my parents or my grandparents, but the dynamic in their family was different, and to me, as a loner for most of my life and someone who had to take full responsibility for herself at an early age, it was refreshing to be exposed to a situation where I could behave and be looked at with accepting and guiding eyes.

Although I was fortunate enough to have these great friends who had great families to look over me and guide me, they were not always around to protect me. After all, I did have my own family in Spain in the form of grandparents whom I would travel to see as regularly as I could. As I said earlier, it was a long trip to their home, which required a full day's travel. I was young and naive, and, on those train rides and bus rides, I was left to fend for myself without the benefit of a guardian to look over me. As we can all recall the innocence of our youth, I was all too trusting and, as a result, an easy target for lessons to be learned.

One such lesson occurred on a particular trip to Bande to meet my grandfather. After taking the train, I had an unusually long wait for the bus transfer to Bande. As I waited for the bus in the terminal, I decided to spend a little time in the cafe adjacent to the terminal to admire the movement of the city. As I sat at a table, a woman dressed in flowing robes, with huge hoop earrings, a scarf over her head and bangle bracelets, approached me and asked if she could share my table. Young and naive, I thought nothing of it and gladly offered her a chair. She began talking to me of travels through Spain and of foreign lands, as though they were neighboring towns. She was a gypsy, nomadic people who never settle in any one place and, also at the time, were known for their predilection for theft among tourists. I thought her harmless enough and continued my conversation with her, inquiring as to her life and travels.

After a while, she leaned over to me and whispered something in my ear softly, as though it were some huge life-changing-epiphany that I was about to be blessed with by her. She said to me, "If you allow me to read your palm, I can tell you what the future holds for you." I was young, naive, and now I had the promise of eternal knowledge. Obviously, I thought, this is too good of an opportunity to pass up. She asked for my hand and looked at my palm. After a brief examination of it, she told me what all of you would expect – generic promises of wealth, fame and happiness. Nonetheless I was exited, and grateful for her knowledge and gift to me. After the reading, we said our goodbyes, and we parted ways amicably. She was off and, as quickly as she came into my life, she was gone.

I sat there for a few moments pondering exactly what had just occurred. A gypsy had come from seemingly nowhere, sat with me and filled my head with stories of parts unknown. She then performed a generic palm reading to create a sense of camaraderie between her and me, and was able to have me lower my guard enough to allow her into my close personal space. She then left in a flash without so much as asking for any sort of compensation for her service. Things were just not adding up in my mind. I began to have this sinking feeling in the pit of my stomach that something just wasn't right with this scenario. So, I reached back to my purse to check my wallet and make sure that everything was still where it was supposed to be, and then it hit me like a ton of bricks. As I opened my wallet, my eyes bright red and filled with desperation, I began to feel a sense of helplessness that I had never felt before. Those very same desperate eyes welled with tears as I finally came to the realization that I had just been robbed blind by the very same damn gypsy who had just promised me eternal fortune. I guess since she saw so much success for my future, I wouldn't need the rest of my bus fare for my trip.

Looking back, it is funny. But at the time, it was a valuable lesson learned about trust. It also served to teach me the old adage that if it seems too good to be true, then it probably is.

There were other numerous events along the way on my travels to my grandparents' house that served to shape me into who I am today. I am sorry to say that these lessons in today's society would be deemed ludicrous to even contemplate, such as the time I abandoned my bus so that I could watch some random guys rehearse with their band after knowing them for all of 10 minutes, but the horrific things that our children must now deal with were not even a consideration for us in those days. Even so, I realized that my childhood innocence was a characteristic that I needed to grow out of quickly.

Earlier, I mentioned that my two friends and their immediate families were the first support system that I had in Spain. Soon after I had returned from Venezuela for my second year of medical training in Spain and my first year of medical school, I met the person who would soon become my primary support system, not only for my time in school and my time in Spain, but for what would become the rest of my life.

It was a day like any other at school. I was in between classes and seated at a table with some friends. We were in the school cafeteria, which was bustling with students and the movement of collegiate life. My friends and I sat down for lunch and were eating peacefully as the room's noise filled the building with life and consumed the halls of the school. One of my friends had had a crush on a particular young man for some time, but had not had the courage to strike up a conversation with him, or share her feelings with this fellow. As luck would have it, the young man walked into the cafeteria on that fateful day with a group of his own friends as we were enjoying our meal. They were older, a few years ahead in the medical curriculum, but they were friendly. We had made it a point to get their attention and have them join our table.

We talked about school and our families in typical get-to-know-you sort of conversation. One guy in particular got my individual attention. His name was Javier Miller. He was a Colombian who had traveled abroad, like me, to attend medical school in Spain. He had, and still has, black curly hair and green eyes, and if you ask him I'm sure he would tell you it was love at first sight. He was particularly nice, and we struck up a good conversation. We exchanged idle chitchat, and, by the time all was said and done, we had made arrangements for him to take me out for dinner. He seemed to be a nice guy. He gave me the impression he was genuine and was someone I might want to get to know a little better. There was another thing that set him apart from all the rest. He had a car, not that it was all that important, but it didn't hurt.

As time went by, school became more demanding, and our relationship grew. Not long after we began dating, I informed him that I suffered from RA. He embraced my situation and was very understanding of it. We began to look for some doctors who might have more experience with cases, such as mine. We also researched some medical regimens that might help me with my pains and symptoms. This became more of a task than I had anticipated, but throughout the entire process he stood by my side, and helped me on my journey to get this nasty disease under control.

Eventually, we found a doctor in A Coruna who was a rheumatologist and specialized in disorders like mine. As mentioned earlier, it is not known exactly what causes RA and, as such, there is no cure for the disease. All of the medical regimens and drugs that had been prescribed to me up until that time were drugs for controlling symptoms. I was hoping that this doctor might have a little more insight as to the root cause of my symptoms and might be able to tackle the problem at a more in-depth level, instead of simply masking the outward symptoms.

A Coruna was about a two-hour drive from Santiago, so we loaded up Javier's car and made our way to the city to see if this doctor could recommend a more decisive and less traumatic course of treatment. The drive there was pretty and picturesque. For the most part, it was farms and mountain views. You could see livestock grazing, and herders tending to goats. There were crops growing as far as the eye could see. Vegetables of all kinds grew on vines and trees, but the view was distorted by the purpose of the trip.

The pain in my joints had been progressing over time, and the swelling had begun to increase to an almost intolerable level. We finally arrived in A Coruna to see this rheumatologist, who after a check up and an overview of my medical history came to the conclusion that I somewhat already knew – I suffered from RA.

Although I had previously known that I had a rheumatological disorder, I did not know the extent of the problem. He sat us down in his office and had a look on his face that I will never forget. I saw in this man what almost seemed to be pity, or empathy, and he had not yet even begun to explain his diagnosis. He informed me that I had RA., which was one of the most severe forms of arthritis that anyone could have. He went on to catalogue the symptoms and side effects that occur as a result of this disease. He told me that in a few years I would be relegated to a wheelchair, which I would be required to use for the rest of my life. Not only that, as I awaited my crippling disfigurement, and prior to being condemned to a wheelchair for the rest of my life, I would need to take extra special precautions while I slept. He required me to sleep with three pillows and to sleep flat on my back. The reason for this was that my disease was so invasive that if I dared to sleep otherwise, my vertebrae would degenerate so rapidly that in my sleep the bones would break and possibly sever my spine. I was 19 years old when this man told me this. I was sitting in his office with my boyfriend, barely beginning my life, and this man just sent my entire world crumbling to its foundation.

I began to cry and feel pity for myself. I wept openly as I could not believe what this man was telling me. He was a noted physician in his field, he had barely examined me, and he knew nothing about the person I was, but in a few short words he had sentenced me to the life of an invalid. He had successfully converted me into an emotional ruin. I had never been faced with my own mortality up to that point, and sadly I let this man who knew nothing of me, force me to call into question the person I was.

Looking back, I'm glad this man said what he did, because I can assure you, I am neither in a wheelchair nor crippled by any means. I am living proof that people are different, and diseases affect people in different ways. This man tried to break me with his words and his alleged superior knowledge, but in retrospect he did not know a damn thing because he treated a diagnosis from a book, not me as a person, and that is not the business I'm in. We, as doctors, treat people, not uniform diseases.

Devastated by his words and crushed by this new development, I began to discuss my previous treatment cycles and the reactions that my body had had to the different drugs. I advised him that I wanted to avoid prednisone due the side effects that I had experienced while taking the drug previously, but I also wanted the most aggressive treatments to delay the onset of any of these dreadful disease-related side effects. I did not tell him about my out-of-body experience, but in retrospect I probably should have, seeing as it was more than likely due to my body and brain chemistry being out of whack.

He recommended a new plan of treatment for the disease. It sounded radical and unorthodox, but who was I to question his advice? After all, he was the expert, and I was desperate for good news, any good news.

There I was, still a teenager, with my boyfriend in tow, and an emotional wreck. Javier tried consoling me, and he did what he could to try and take my mind off the dreadful prognosis that had just been given to me. But sometimes in life there just aren't any words that can heal such deep wounds. We sat in the office trying to put up the appearance of a unified front, but inside I was demolished. Javier just listened and held me. It seemed as though he knew there were no words that could ease what I had just experienced.

Upon further conversation with this "specialist," he devised a plan of action for my treatment. This plan called for me to undergo a self-injection therapy that consisted of a mixture of gold salts. I had never heard of this form of therapy, but at this point in time I was willing to try anything to alleviate the excruciating pain of this debilitating disease and prolong the onset of any further effects. He described the treatment and informed me that it came as a series of injections that I would have to give myself in my buttocks over a certain period of time. The gold salts were supposed to work like anti-inflammatory drugs, but they were not supposed to have the same side effects that the prednisone had had on my body. I was relieved to learn that these gold salts would not cause any of the bleeding or the associated weight gain from the previous treatment, but I was then met with the unfortunate news of all of the other burdens carried by these drugs.

The doctor informed me first of the serious nature of the side effects that the gold salts could possibly carry. These included, but were not limited to, all sorts of kidney disease and damage, as well as urinary infections that varied in severity from mild to full kidney failure. I was concerned, but I also was willing to take the advice to heart and was willing to try anything to ease the pain. The next bit of information this gentleman provided was something that I had not expected. He told us that he would write a prescription for the gold salts, but we would not be able to fill the prescription in Spain. We would have to drive across the border into Portugal in order to fill the prescription, then smuggle the medication back into Spain. I say smuggle, but to my knowledge it was not illegal at the time to possess these gold salts. I just knew that I could not obtain them legally within the country.

Armed with my prescriptions and my boyfriend at my side, we drove the hour and change to the border that was very close to Santiago and to the nearest town in order to fill the prescriptions for these gold salts. Just like the drive to A Coruna, the road was marked by small villages and farmland near and far. The mountain views were spectacular, but we never took the time to really enjoy them as we had a singular purpose in mind. Our clandestine mission was to get into Portugal, find the nearest pharmacy, fill the prescriptions and get out of Portugal as quick as possible. It sounds like the makings of a spy novel, but, for me, it was really a matter of grave importance, as I now saw this treatment as a cure for my pain.

We got in and out of Portugal without any hassle, and were able to find the medicine fairly uneventfully. I was able to communicate with the people, as Gallego, my grandmother's language, was almost identical to Portuguese. When we returned to the border we were met with no questions, and we continued on our way back to school. To say that our adventures to and from the appointments and over the border were fun would be untrue, but it was refreshing to know that there was someone there with me. For the first time, I began to feel as though I was not alone, and I began to appreciate the shoulder that I was able to lean on during these times.

Things did not end there with the adventure of the gold salts. After our return to Santiago with the vials of medication, I realized that I actually had to stab my own flesh with a needle and put this stuff into my body. I know it sounds ridiculous, but I have never, ever, been a fan of needles. To know that I had to inject myself was torture, so I did the only logical thing that I could. I made Javier do the injections instead. I continued to go to the lab to check my blood, I would take iron shots for my anemia, and I would also take the gold salts for the RA. After research and subsequent visits to the rheumatologist in A Coruna, I tinkered and toyed with almost every single anti-inflammatory drug known to man. The pains persisted, the aches persisted, and the agony and mental anguish began to take hold on me. I began to wonder what I had done to deserve this agonizing life sentence. The mental toll began to be as unbearable as the physical toll that the disease was exacting on my body.

Life went on and school went on, as well. I had progressed through the program with ease, since that unfortunate academic incident in my first medical school year. Grades were going well, I had friends, and my relationship was wonderful. I had already introduced Javier to my family in Orense, and we had gone on a few trips to my grandparents' house together. The trips were long, but now they were made easier by the fact that I no longer had to ride the train and bus to get to their home.

These trips were much more tolerable in a car than they were on the bus, and I was more able to appreciate the beauty and the landscape of northern Spain in the solitude of these rides. Snow would fall in the mountains, to create a blanket that would cover the earth. This sight was beautiful, except for the time when we got three flat tires on the way and had to walk in thigh-high snow to finally reach my grandparents' home. In the summer the fields would be alive with crops and livestock. Things were going well, and life could not have been better for us at the time.

In the fall of 1977, my life took another unexpected, but welcome, turn. Javier and I had been in a relationship for a few years already, and he had been an incredible partner. He had supported me and helped me through the difficult times of my disease, and he understood my situation in relation to my studies. We had fun together, and things had turned serious for us. He proposed and, just like that, I was engaged to be married. Like every little girl, I had always dreamed of the day I would get married with the ceremony, the dress and all of the other things about which we girls dream. I immediately informed my family of the engagement, and was met with warmth and support.

My mother and sister flew from Venezuela to help me find my perfect dress, as well as to finalize all of the planning. We were married on January 6, 1978, in the Catholic Cathedral in Santiago de Compostella. It was still cold out, but it was a beautiful day nonetheless. My grandparents, as well as some uncles, came from Orense to witness our nuptials. It was a small ceremony with us being surrounded by family and some friends, but it was exactly what anyone could have asked for. The entire day, I felt like a fairy-tale princess, and at the end of the day I had found my prince who would share my side for the rest of my life. The ceremony was traditional, and the reception was a small but raucous gathering. You can imagine the damage that a few farmers and some college students can do. It was picture perfect and, as many of you can relate, a memory that I will forever cherish.

Javier graduated in 1978, but I was still in school. He was now looking for work as a doctor in the area and found a job in a hospital as a surgical trainee in A Coruna. The only problem was that this was almost a two-hour drive from Santiago where the medical school was located. The good thing about this job opportunity was that the hospital he would be working at was a short walk from the clinic where I would be doing my final rotations. We also lucked out in the sense that the hospital was willing to give us a room to stay in as a residence, while he worked and I finished school. It worked out perfectly, and things could not have been better.

I was nearing my last year of school, when life threw another variable into our mix. Shortly after I began my final year of medical school, I received the wonderful news that I was pregnant.

Pregnant! I was 22, married, about to finish medical school and now pregnant. Looking back, this was a wonderful period in my life, but at the time I was terrified—not because I was pregnant, but because I had no idea how my disease would affect my unborn child.

I tried to research as much information as I could on RA and its effects on both the pregnant mother, as well as the unborn child.

Unfortunately, there was no real literature on the topic. Due to the relatively mysterious nature of the disease itself, and the relative scarcity on causes and effective treatments, I could not find any answers to any of my questions. I had no idea how RA would affect me as a pregnant mother. Would it cause more severe flare-ups? Would it cause constant chronic pains? Would it complicate or exacerbate any underlying dormant issues internally? More importantly and at the forefront of my concerns was how would it affect my unborn child? Would my anemia somehow create nutritional issues during the pregnancy? Would my arthritis cause some unforeseen and perhaps catastrophic turn in my pregnancy? These were questions that nobody could answer for me, and they were questions that I was unwilling to gamble my child's life on. I read studies, I researched what I could, and as time went by I started feeling some changes in my body.

I never got any major questions answered from my research, but Mother Nature sure began to answer some questions herself without the need for any fancy studies or tests. I began to notice, as my pregnancy progressed, a decrease in pain, a lower level of swelling, and aches and soreness that women would associate with pregnancy instead of arthritis. My flare-ups were less severe, almost to the point that they entirely disappeared. My back was sore, but that was from my new belly and not another manifestation of the disease itself. It was almost as if being pregnant was the best cure or treatment plan that I had ever encountered for my RA. Since diagnosed at the age of 18, I had never felt so healthy and pain free, as I did when I was pregnant.

Today, there are theories for this manifestation and the curative effects of pregnancy, but, as previously stated, just like there is no known cause of RA, experts don't exactly know why or what causes a decrease in the effects of the disease during pregnancy. It is also not a given that every sufferer of RA will have a similar experience while pregnant as I did. There are some statistics that indicate there are a percentage of women, like me, who experience curative responses, some experience no change, and a small number of women will experience an intensification of their symptoms. I was one of the lucky ones in the first group.

As previously mentioned, there is no direct link as to why the body fights the disease better while pregnant, but some studies have indicated a possible link between the increased hormone levels during pregnancy as a possible cause for this phenomenon. During pregnancy the body increases its production of progesterone, estrogen and countless other hormones that react within the body. These natural hormones act sort of in the same way as the earlier medication I was taking, prednisone, in the respect that they are natural anti-inflammatory hormones without the nasty side effects of the medications.

I was ecstatic that things were going the way they were with regards to the pregnancy, but school was tough as was getting used to the work schedules of a practicing physician, which Javier now was. In those days, there was no residency program as there is now. What Javier was doing was shadowing surgeons and assisting them with operations. Once he had completed three years of this on-the-job training he would have been qualified to practice as a surgeon in Spain, but that was not the plan.

The plan was always to return to South America and rejoin our parents. Since Columbia and Venezuela were neighboring countries, the travel between the two locations was simple enough, and if we settled in either we knew we were close enough to the other for short trips, as both countries were easily accessible to each other. In the end, through a series of events that I will describe later in the chapter, we decided to settle in Venezuela near my parents.

Before we could make any such move, I had to finish my medical training and receive my diploma so that I would be eligible to practice medicine back in Venezuela, as well. This was all well in theory, but in practice it proved difficult. The stress of studying, as well as the stress of pregnancy was gradually becoming quite a heavy load to carry.

Thrown in were bits of great news. At the hospital where my husband was working, we were able to get pregnancy-related health care and, in one of our visits with the doctor, he was able to tell us the gender of our first child. It was a boy. We were so excited and as happy as could be. We settled on a name early on and decided that he was going to be a junior.

Somehow we managed to handle work, school and pregnancy, as well as all of the other issues that face newly married couples. We pushed through as our own little family support system, and things were going well for us in our little world. In 1979, I graduated from medical school and was bestowed the title of Medical Doctor by the Universidad de Santiago de Compostella. This was not the greatest event to happen in 1979 for our family though. On June 11, 1979, I went into labor and, after several hours of pain and pushing, into the world came the most perfect little thing that we had ever laid eyes on. Javier Miller Jr. was born that day, and it was the most gratifying and happiest day of my life. To see those eyes, and that face, and that beautiful healthy baby boy, it only stood to re-affirm everything that my husband and I had been doing and striving for up until that point, and it also marked the exciting beginning of our family.

Now, I was a recent graduate, a wife of not more than two years, and a mother. After the birth of our child, we took a slow approach towards our next step. Javier had completed almost two years of his surgical training, and only needed one more year of training until he had completed all the necessary requirements to practice and be licensed as a surgeon. There was nothing to keep us in Spain though. We had accomplished all that we had moved there to accomplish; we both graduated, we were married, and our child had been born healthy. I did not want to begin any training programs in Spain if those programs would be cut short because we were going to return to Venezuela anyway. I did not want to have to begin, cut a program off and then be forced to begin training all over again after being unable to complete at least a year of training.

We faced another problem, as well. Javier still lacked that last year of surgery he needed to qualify him as a surgeon. After our son was born, we began looking into positions in Venezuela, and sending our colleagues in Venezuela correspondence making them aware of our current situation. This process extended for several months. All the while, I lived the life of a stay-at-home mom taking care of our infant son, while Javier continued his training. Javier Jr. continued to grow and was, for the most part, a healthy baby boy. He was a bit colicky, which made him a little sick as a young baby, but generally he fed well, he slept well, and was about as healthy a baby as we could have asked for.

After about six months and some considerable back and forth with friends, colleagues, and officials, we received some good news from representatives of the government of Venezuela. Somehow, they had been alerted to our situation, and the ministry of education took this opportunity to extend an invitation and an acceptance of my husband's foreign medical training. They were in need of physicians with surgical experience and offered him a position as a surgeon with full credentials in the country. The news came in the form of an official letter from the government of Venezuela addressed to my husband with the name of the hospital to which he was to report once he arrived in the country. It appeared to be the fairy-tale beginning for which we were hoping. Things were settled, we were going to return to Venezuela, and we were going to begin our lives surrounded by family and support, or so we thought!

CHAPTER 4

"Minds are like parachutes, they only work when they are open."
—*ANONYMOUS*

Finally our hard work had paid off, and our persistence was being validated by the government of Venezuela with their offer of acceptance of our credentials. We celebrated the good news with friends in Spain, and we began to prepare ourselves for the journey to our new home. We did all of the necessary things in order to prepare for the move. We informed our employers, we informed all of our friends, and we packed what amounted to our entire lives in a few little boxes for the long trip across the Atlantic.

We had time before we needed to be in Venezuela, as there was no official start date in the letter we received. Actually, the only thing the letter said was to report to the ministry of education upon our arrival, and things would be sorted out from there. Armed with this knowledge, we decided to grant ourselves a little bit of a treat and planned a trip to the United States to see Javier's aunt and uncle who lived in New York City. We made the arrangements, sent our belongings to Venezuela and embarked on our trip home, with a short stopover in what, at the time, for many was considered the land of opportunity and dreams, America.

In September 1979, I left Spain for the last time. I had arrived years before as a frightened little girl with no money in my pockets, without a clear plan as to what my future was going to look like, or be. On this date, I left a confident woman. I was married, I had a son, and I was a doctor. I had accomplished everything I had set out to accomplish in Spain, and I was grateful for the experience. The time I spent in Spain, I believe, made me the person that I am today. I discovered so much about myself in those few short years. I discovered my disease, I discovered my resolve, I discovered my husband, and I created my family. I have nothing but fond memories of those days, and whenever I look back upon them an instant smile breaks out across my face.

There were mixed emotions when we left Spain. We had created so many memories for ourselves, and we had fought so hard for what little we had, but our plan was always to return to our families. This chapter in our lives was about to close, and looking back was nostalgia and fond memories, but a new chapter in the book of our lives was opening up, and awaiting us was excitement and opportunity.

Javier, Javier Jr. and I arrived in the United States in September 1979 at New York City's LaGuardia Airport. As we landed and I could see the city, its sheer size and all of the flashing lights, I was immediately drawn to it. We were met in the airport by Javier's aunt and uncle, who welcomed us into their home for our mini vacation. While in New York, we took a walking tour of Manhattan, and I was immediately sucked in by the energy and vitality of the people, as well as the life and presence of the city itself. It was beautiful to witness as a tourist, but I remember thinking how overwhelming it would be to live there.

We were also fortunate enough to be able to make the relatively short drive over to Niagara Falls during our stay in the U.S. I remember taking in the breathtaking vistas offered by this natural wonder, but I could not help but think towards the future awaiting us at our new home. After a week of sightseeing in America, we were ready to make the final leg of our journey to Venezuela. We said our goodbyes to family, and we boarded a plane bound for Caracas, Venezuela.

The United States had left a great impression on me. I remember leaving and thinking that I would love to come back some day and see more of the country as a tourist. I never dreamt that things were going to turn out the way they did, and, eventually one day, this would be the place that I called home.

We arrived in Caracas and immediately hit the ground running in order to put things in order, so that we could begin working and get ourselves settled as quickly as possible.

We made arrangements prior to arriving in the country for a place to stay briefly in Caracas while sorting out our academic credentials. Before leaving Spain, Javier had a patient in the hospital in A Coruna who had been the victim of a domestic-violence shooting. She arrived in the hospital in critical condition after suffering a gunshot wound to the spine. She was immediately paralyzed by the incident and required numerous surgeries, as well as prolonged care. Javier was part of the surgical team that was able not only to save this woman's life, but was also integral in nursing her back to health, as well as assisting her in adjusting to her new life.

This unfortunate woman was a Venezuelan national living in Spain. Throughout the time of her care, she discovered that Javier and I were soon to be moving to her home country. After conversation and months of care, she grew a bond with Javier and me, and eventually offered her assistance in making our move to Venezuela as smooth and seamless as could be. She approached us one day and offered her apartment in Caracas for us to use while we were in the capital verifying our credentials. We accepted the offer, and for three days after our arrival we made her apartment our home.

After three days in the capital, and a lot of back and forth, we finally were able to establish that the people we needed to speak with would be at the local ministry of education in the state where we would be living.

My father drove to Caracas, picked us up, and drove us to the state of Tachira, where we would make our permanent home. Tachira was also the state where my parents made their final home, and upon our arrival I was finally reunited with my mother and my sister. My parents opened their home to us, and allowed us to make ourselves comfortable under their roof. We were a bit anxious to get our affairs in order in our new home, and we were also filled with mixed emotions from our experience in Caracas.

We did not have any real answers, and an overwhelming sense of uncertainty surrounded us as we tried to get definitive responses from government officials regarding acceptance of our degrees and training. Once in Tachira, we were directed to the local office for the ministry of education. When we arrived, we were then re-directed to another office in a neighboring state. At this point, I began to wonder exactly what was happening, and why we couldn't get a straight answer from any officials or government representatives. Again, we were turned away as if we were a burden, and told that the answers that we sought were located at the ministry of education in Merida, the neighboring Venezuelan state.

I will provide a little background in the history of South America, particularly with regards to my experiences in Colombia and Venezuela. South America in the late 1970s and early 1980s was a very dynamic place. Around this time there was an explosion in the consumption, as well as production, of cocaine. The drug comes from the leaves of the coca plant, and is processed significantly with chemicals and other means. The resulting product is a fine white powder that can be either snorted through the nostrils, or smoked in a rock form. The leading producer of the product at the time was Colombia, the neighboring country to Venezuela. The drug business was and still is a quite lucrative one, and as such can also be quite a violent business. As I previously said, the time we were moving to South America was at the height of the drug boom, and intuitively made the situation a significantly more dangerous time to be relocating to the area.

The drug epidemic, along with its accompanying violence, was a serious issue we were facing already, but along with that there were secondary issues that threatened our smooth transition to our new lives. There has always been a grass-roots-resistance-pseudo-revolutionary movement in South America. There had been revolutionaries fighting in the jungles and villages of the countryside throughout the continent in many of the countries of South America for a very long time. As such, there was a heightened and visible military presence. These armed guerilla groups were fighting in the name of different causes and in different eras.

With the explosion of the drug trade, a new revenue stream emerged. These groups were not ones to rest on their laurels and quickly became major players in this new enterprise. Now these groups were armed with money, as well as with a cause that they were willing to die to defend, and the military of these countries were on heightened alert. The state of things was noticeable, and there were armed soldiers everywhere the eye could see. There was a military presence at the airport when we arrived in Caracas. There were military checkpoints randomly scattered throughout the city. There were military checkpoints located at every border crossing from state to state within Venezuela, as well as an even higher military presence located at the borders with neighboring countries, such as Colombia.

At these checkpoints, we would be subject to search, as well as required to provide documentation as to exactly who we were and what our business was traveling on the path that we were going. It was really intimidating and a stark difference from the life that we were accustomed to in Spain. This is not to say that life in Spain didn't have its difficulties as well, but, while living in Europe, we were not used to seeing so much military activity and hearing of so many violent crimes occurring daily. Needless to say, it was a culture shock, and it was going to take some getting used to.

Armed with the news that we were again required to go to yet another government office and try to validate our credentials there, we departed from my parents' house leaving little Javier with my parents as we made our way across the state border. On our way there, we had to cross what amounted to about four military police checks. Each time it was the same process, stop the car and allow the soldiers to search if they so desired. After any searches be prepared to hand over all of your paperwork, which included passport, any official documents proving where you were going, any licenses you were carrying, basically anything that proved you were who you said you were, and you were going to where you said you were going. It was intrusive and, at times, a little degrading in the sense that some of these men had little else to do other than give you a hard time, and in so doing they spoke to you as if you were scum foreigners who were beneath them. Theirs was a thankless job, and they did not do much else to change that perception. I do not mean to paint with a broad brush, but those select few soldiers stationed at these checkpoints who wanted to make your life miserable at each turn made an impression that colored my perception of the whole lot.

We finally arrived at the office of the ministry of education in Merida after what seemed an eternity, but in reality was only a few hours drive. Once there we signed in to let the official, who was to review our paperwork, know that we had arrived. It was a surreal feeling hoping that this could possibly be the end of our long journey, but we were both optimistic that things would go well. After a little while waiting in the lobby for the official to call us back for review, we were finally escorted into an office where we met a gentleman who identified himself as the man in charge. My husband and I looked at each other and released a collective sigh, realizing that we had finally reached a person who could give us some answers. He invited us to sit, before commencing the conversation of our future posts and rights.

From the beginning of the meeting, there was an uncomfortable air to the entire scene. We were asked about our past and our families, we were asked about our reasons for wanting to move to Venezuela, we were asked about our medical training and our experience in Spain. Everything was covered, but the entire interview seemed as though there was something being hidden from us. Any time we asked about our credentials, the question was deflected. Any time we asked about our post or how soon we could begin working in Tachira, the topic was quickly changed. This went on for several minutes, almost an hour, when, in an attempt to receive some concrete answers, we finally inquired about the letter that my husband had received from the government.

This was when the 10-ton brick was dropped on us. The official reached across the desk and took the letter from Javier's hands. He sat back in his chair and leisurely read the contents of the letter. He leaned forward, placed the letter flat on his desk, and proceeded to crush all of our hopes, dreams, and, to that point, our current aspirations. He looked at us with a menacing smirk, and said, "Well, this letter has no value." Our response came out immediately, "What do you mean no value?" He replied that since the government had changed hands, and the previous government's officials had written the letter guaranteeing our position and acceptance, this letter had no meaning to the current government in power. We were devastated, we had left our home, the only place we knew as home as a family, we left our friends, we left our jobs, all on account of this stupid little letter. We thought it was our ticket back to reuniting with our families and beginning our careers, and now this man sat before us, with a demonic smirk and in two sentences crushed our entire being.

We both cringed, but determined Javier responded that this could not be. How could they turn away two doctors, when there was such an obvious need in the country for healthcare professionals? The response we received next was worse than the initial news. The official said, "You both misunderstand me, we are not going to turn you away ..." A sense of momentary relief settled into both of us as he continued, "No, we won't turn you away, you are right in the sense that the country needs doctors ..." OK, we looked at each other wondering where he was going with this, "But if you want to practice medicine in this country, you and your wife are going to be sent to the most remote parts of the Amazon jungle to provide healthcare to patients in the frontier land," he said. You could feel the air being sucked out of the room.

Our son was only a few months old, we came to the country to be near family, and we needed their help in getting ourselves situated. Here, this man was telling us that this was all for nothing. He was going to send us into the jungle, days away from contact with civilization and nowhere near our families to practice in some of the most dangerous parts of the world. It was basically a way of telling us we were not welcome here, and good luck elsewhere. The state had just given us an option, which really was no option at all. We looked at each other defeated and dejected, we thanked the man for his time, and we made our way towards the door of his office. As we were leaving the meeting, he so kindly reminded us that the only option to practice medicine in *his* country, and at this point it really did feel like he owned the country, was to relocate to the jungle. We thanked him again for his time, and politely excused ourselves from his office.

We sat in the car on the verge of tears. We had left everything, we had nothing in this country except our dreams, and now those were in jeopardy. We discussed relocation, but it just seemed impossible with such a young child and just so out of our element. On our drive back to my parents' house, the topic kept coming up, and we began to discuss it more in depth. That all stopped and our minds were made up after a few short minutes at a military checkpoint on our way home from that fateful meeting.

We were leaving Merida, which is near the Colombia/Venezuela border and where the meeting took place, and heading home to Tachira, a neighboring state where my parents lived. Colombia and Venezuela have always had an interesting relationship and, at the time, relations were strained over the illegal immigration of Colombians into Venezuela to find work and means of survival. Undocumented Colombians had been crossing the border in order to work days in Venezuela and take money back home to support their families. Unfortunately, as with any criminal enterprise, there were some salacious activities occurring near the border as well. At the time, smugglers had found it lucrative to sneak white Colombian women over the border and sell them into slavery and prostitution through a complex network of human trafficking. Apparently this was a very common occurrence, and the military had been put on high alert to look out for this type of activity on the border.

So, my Colombian husband and I found ourselves returning from a border town alone right around sunset, a perfect time for criminal activity. We approached a military checkpoint, just like we had on our way in, but there must have been a guard change because none of the soldiers from earlier were at this post now. A soldier approached the car and tapped on the window with the butt of his weapon. Javier lowered the window, and was as polite as possible to the soldier and greeted him respectfully. From that point we knew there seemed as if something was out of place. These usually tense encounters had an elevated and almost extreme tension surrounding us, and the other soldiers also stationed here seemed to be extremely irritable gripping their machine guns with a vulture-like hand upon them. The man demanded our paperwork, which we gladly gave over to him. We gave our passports, a copy of our diplomas, and the letter indicating where we were coming from.

On top of the stack was my husband's Colombian passport. Once the soldier saw that, he immediately summoned the other soldiers over, and yelled "Colombian." The other soldiers arrived almost in a sprint. Flashlights went on, and they immediately started flashing them into the car. "He's got a girl with him," one of the others yelled, and then I felt a feeling that I will never forget, and I would not wish upon anyone in this world. I had, to that point, never held a gun, let alone shot a gun in my life. I knew nothing about guns, but this feeling was unmistakably terrifying. I felt the cold steel opening of the barrel of a machine gun pressed against my head. I screamed. They panicked, screaming back, calling my husband and me all sorts of names. We went into panic mode, and this only served to scare and infuriate these soldiers, as well. The original soldier dropped our paperwork and reached for his gun. Javier instinctively reached over to try to pick the papers up, so he could show them my passport and explain that I was his wife. The soldier screamed and told him not to move or they would kill us both. We both froze, we were helpless, and at the mercy of these bastards, defenseless and terrified. After what seemed an eternity, but was likely seconds, everyone began to catch their breath, and Javier calmly explained who he was. He told them he was a doctor returning from a meeting in Merida with the ministry of education regarding a training position. He then went on to explain that I was his wife. He assured them I was not a prostitute and he was not a smuggler. He showed them our passports, he showed them a copy of our diplomas, and he showed them the government letter. All the while, I still had a gun to my head, with what appeared to be a teenage trigger-happy lunatic holding the trigger. I was terrified, and all I could think about was my son, my family, and the future that was going to be taken away from me by this animal. Javier continued explaining our situation, but it did not seem to be convincing them.

Finally, a superior came over and exchanged words with the soldiers asking what was going on, with the gun still pointed directly at my head. When the first soldier came back, he handed Javier the paperwork and said only, "Go." No other words were exchanged, and our papers were thrown back into the car at us. When the man standing at my window with the gun to my head removed it, he leaned in and said something to me that I can still hear being whispered into my ear to this day. He leaned in and said, "You were saved by the bell, this time."

I have no idea what he meant by it, but I can still feel the heat from his breath and those terrifying words being uttered to this day. We rolled up our windows as they raised the barricade to let us pass, and we drove as if we had stolen that car. When finally out of sight and far enough away, we stopped the car and shared our terror from the incident. We realized how quickly things could be taken from us and shared an embrace. We realized how little we actually controlled, and how much less we controlled here in this country. To compare our prior lives in Spain, and pit that against what we had seen as our future lives in Venezuela, we just could not bring ourselves to accept it.

That was the point when we realized we could not live there, and that our future extended beyond the boundaries of that country. We could not live in constant fear and uncertainty. We refused to raise our son in a place where we could not guarantee his safety because, to a great extent, it was out of our hands. When we collected ourselves and arrived back at my parents' house, we sat down and basically tried to decide upon our plan of action. We had left Spain to be close to family, and we had sold everything off back there, so a return to Europe was out of the question. Javier's entire family lived in Colombia, which was the next door neighbor to Venezuela. His family was large and had been established in Colombia for generations. His father was a physician who had many ties to the local community, and the country was close in proximity to where my family lived. A logical path, and the path we decided to pursue, was to travel to Colombia and explore any opportunities that there may be there.

We made arrangements to travel, and meet with government representatives to explore our options in Colombia. A few weeks after our incident at the checkpoint, we set off for Colombia to see if we would be a good fit there. Unfortunately, the situation in Colombia was bleak. There was no job opportunity for us, and although we would have the support of family, we would not have the luxury of practicing our craft. Also, there was the very real threat of danger ever present in Colombia. Kidnappings were on the rise, and the government was embroiled in a decades-long battle with revolutionary forces in the jungles of the rural villages. On top of those struggles, drug cartels were battling each other for precious turf and drug markets, resulting in the violent deaths of thousand of people annually.

The reason we left Venezuela and decided to search Colombia was because of violence and to try to settle somewhere where we could raise our son in relative safety. To make a move to a country that was just as badly off as Venezuela would have been ludicrous in our minds. We returned to Venezuela again defeated. We didn't know where to turn. We both felt depressed and dejected, and we were just searching for some direction.

That is when Javier made a decision that would change the course of our lives forever. When Javier was a child, his father worked as a physician in Tampa, Florida. His entire family had lived there except for Javier. He had left home to pursue medicine in Spain at the age of 16, and soon thereafter his father decided to uproot the family in search of a better life in the United States. His father was able to apply for resident status for Javier and his siblings who were minors, and Javier accepted the arrangement so that he could go to Tampa over the summers to visit his family and work to save up spending money for the school year. After a few years, his family decided that they missed their homeland and returned to Colombia, but they all still had their U.S. green cards.

Javier decided that we were going to move to America, the land of the free and the home of the brave. I had never thought that I would ever have the opportunity to live in the United States. At the time, living in the U.S. was a dream that everyone wanted to somehow one day achieve, but there were a few problems. First, even though my husband had resident status, my son and I did not. Second, even if we could get paperwork to gain entry to the country, where would we live? Third, the reason we moved away from Spain to South America was solely to be close to our families. The only family we had in America was Javier's aunt who lived in New York. Last, and probably most importantly, neither one of us spoke a word of English.

Undeterred, Javier was adamant that our future did not include South America any longer, and if we were going to survive and thrive we had to move to the U.S. Logistically getting my paperwork for residency was a bit of a problem. We had set up our temporary home base in Venezuela with my parents, but since my husband was a Colombian citizen with U.S. residency, the application and paperwork had to be filled out and turned in at the Consulate office in Bogotá, Colombia. So off we went to Colombia again, this time in an attempt to expedite my entry to the U.S.A. The flight was short, but the ramifications of our journey were massive. Still, we knew we were making the right choice. If we were to have any sort of future and provide any form of opportunity for our child, we had to make this move. Once in Bogotá, things went smoothly, we stayed with some family members and made our way to the U.S. embassy. We filled out all of the necessary paperwork, and were told that we should hear back from the U.S. government in a few months.

After our short stay in Colombia, we felt confident that our application for residency would be approved without incident, but then a whole new set of problems arose. What were we going to do when we reached America? Then we realized that what we were going to do was not the most pressing matter. The most pressing matter was where we were going to live. I did not know the country at all, I knew that we flew into New York once, and then flew out, but if you asked me any questions regarding U.S. geography it would have been like asking an infant to do a calculus problem. Javier had a little bit of exposure to the U.S. on his visits to see his family during the summers, but that was limited to the central Florida area.

Upon our return to Venezuela, we discussed where we would try to settle initially. We settled on Miami. Miami seemed like a good choice for many reasons. It was the first port of entry from South America, so it would be the shortest flight over. There was a huge Hispanic population in the city, so it would be a little easier than other places to become acclimated to the country. Plus, it was a fairly large city, so we should be able to find work there while we figured out how to validate our medical credentials in our new home.

So that was settled, we were moving to Miami. Or should I say Javier was moving to Miami. When we came to this decision, I had yet to hear from the U.S. consulate in Colombia with regards to my immigration status. I had no idea how long it would take, but my husband and I also realized that we couldn't wait until the last minute and just up and go to a new country with an infant son, and no plan as to how we would support ourselves there. So in July 1980, Javier boarded a plane and flew to Miami, alone.

Once he arrived in Miami, he did everything in his power to set up a nice family home for us, so that we could feel cozy when we came over, as well. He found a small one-bedroom apartment in Miami, with a kitchen and living space. It wasn't much, but for us it was perfect. He found a job at Coral Reef hospital moonlighting and assisting in basically whatever he was needed to do in the hospital. If the trash had to go out, he would volunteer, if they needed him to help in surgery, he was their man. He was basically their go-to guy for anything and everything, and they appreciated someone like him who was so eager to help. He worked all different shifts and never complained at all to the higher ups. He took medical histories, and in doing so worked on improving his English. The people at the hospital really took note of this, and it turned out to be a really great fit.

All the while my husband was working and trying to prepare everything for our arrival in Miami, I finally received word from Bogotá with regards to my residency status. I was to return for my final interview, and then I would hear word within a few weeks if my application was granted or not. I immediately made my arrangements for my return to Colombia. Javier Jr. and I boarded one of the first flights we could, and packed for an extended stay in Colombia so that we could be there when we found out the news.

I stayed with a distant aunt of my husband's in Bogotá, a kind and loving older lady. She opened her home to my son and me without any hesitation, and welcomed us for the duration of our stay. I attended the final interview at the consulate, and was very pleased with the outcome. The representative was friendly, and outgoing, which gave me a positive perspective for my chances of being approved. He thanked me for coming and informed me that we should have a final decision within a few weeks.

So, with all of the paperwork submitted and all of the face-to-face interviews completed, I basically had only one choice now – hurry up and wait. I volunteered to help Merceditas, Javier's aunt, with any and all chores around the house. I would help her carry the groceries and help with cleaning around the house. I would do anything and everything to make myself useful, but she was so sweet that she would tell me to relax, make myself at home and worry about caring for my son. She even helped me with that. It was a wonderful time, but during that period I was yet again reminded about why my husband and I had made the decision that we did to leave the country.

One day, I was out for a walk with my son and Merceditas. We decided to take a stroll through the park and enjoy the beautiful day that we were experiencing. The sky was blue, and there were people lounging, restfully in the park. We were in conversation, me holding my son in my arms and Merceditas to my side. We had fallen into such an interesting conversation that, for the most part, we were unaware of our surroundings. I stopped for a moment as we continued speaking when all of a sudden I felt a large hand grasp the back of my neck. I froze in a panicked shock. The hand wrapped around my neck and violently ripped at a small gold chain that I was wearing that day. I screamed as loud as I could, fearing that this man might cause harm to either myself or, worse still, my child. I protectively wrapped my entire body around my son trying to shield him from the stranger. The man ran off when he heard my screams, but in broad daylight in the middle of the park nobody even moved or attempted to give us any help. Those were the times we were living in, and that was the reality from which my husband and I decided to flee.

After that incident, I rarely left Merceditas' house and if I did it was alone. I never took my son outside, and we avoided any trips that would require us to walk for any extended distances. I was frightened after the incident, and with all of the violence and terrible things that had been occurring I refused to take a chance with my son outdoors. Finally, after two months of waiting, I heard back from the U.S. consulate. They sent a letter to the house, in a sealed thick envelope. I looked at the envelope and hesitated for a moment before I opened it. I sat there staring at the envelope and my child, realizing that our entire hopes, all of our dreams, and our entire future would likely one way or another be determined by whatever was contained inside of it. The emotion of the moment was gargantuan, and I had to compose myself before looking inside.

I finally brought myself to the point where I just tore the thing open and reached in, ripping the contents out in one swift motion. I looked down and began to read impatiently to see what lay ahead for us. Once I got midway through the page, I saw it staring back at me; there it was in print and in my hand. I had been granted resident status to the United States of America, and I was going to live in the land of opportunity. We were going to raise our family in America. The thing that only a few short years ago, seemed to be something that was unattainable was staring back at me right in my face. I had never imagined that this day would come, but it was here, and I was overjoyed. Emotions took hold of me, and I grabbed my son and hugged him as hard as I could. I was elated, and I was celebrating for the entire world to hear. I called Javier and told him the great news. We were happy, and now we were ready for the next leg of our journey.

Javier Jr. and I left Bogotá and returned to Venezuela so that I could get the remainder of our things. I packed our bags and we made arrangements for our flight to Miami. In the midst of all of this happiness and emotion, I lost track of one thing. I had not had time to think about the fact that I would again be leaving my parents and family, only this time I was leaving them for good. Javier and I had made a decision to move to America to practice medicine there and raise our family there. We had effectively ruled out a return to South America in the future, and, in reality, we had never even brought up the topic of a return. The reality of the situation began to take hold and a sudden sadness enveloped me. In September 1980, my son and I boarded a plane bound for Miami, Florida. I said my good-byes to my parents and my sister, knowing that the original plan that we had masterminded when I was just a little girl leaving for Spain would never come true. I would never return to live near them and raise my children near their grandparents. My husband had that same realization. We were embarking on a journey that neither of us had ever dreamed was going to be part of our lives, but nonetheless it was a necessary evil. We had to escape to somewhere that offered us a chance, somewhere where we knew that if we wanted it bad enough we could find success, and there was just one place where this could be a reality. The emotions of the day were mixed, but there was a definite sadness. Just as quickly as we had arrived, we were now gone, alone again, for good this time.

While in South America for those few short months, my husband and I learned a lot about ourselves. First, we learned a lot about our resilience and our willingness to make tough decisions work for us. We learned that if we worked together, we could come up with some really amazing and difficult understandings about things that affected our realities. Most importantly for me, I began to notice some interesting characteristics about my health and my disease. I noticed that my disease began to regress, or lay dormant while we were back in South America. Why that was exactly, I still had no idea. I was still taking anti-inflammatory medications, but I was taking them in lower doses, and the violent flare ups that had plagued me in Spain were all but non-existent while there.

I never really thought about why that was, but then we really did not have much time to wonder about such things. Maybe one of the reasons could have been that we were under so much stress that my body was just masking the pain from itself as it does when someone feels a rush of adrenaline. Whatever the reason I had no clue, but I also was never one to be an ungrateful recipient of a gift. So, with my RA in check and all of the nasty and terrifying memories from the last few months erased from my mind, we embarked on our journey to our new home.

The flight over was generally uneventful, and once Javier Jr. and I arrived we were greeted by my husband at the gate. We shared an embrace, and he welcomed us to our new home. We made our way down to baggage claim, as he filled us in on all that had happened over the previous two months while he was there. He told me about the job he had found at the hospital, and described the vast array of responsibilities that he had there. He let me know about the good experience he was getting, and how much practice he was receiving with his English. At this point, it hit me that I had to learn how to speak English, I asked myself, "How the hell am I going to learn how to speak English?" "Well," I thought, "I can leave that task for another day." At this point, I was just happy that our journey was over, and we were finally reunited. After getting the luggage, we made our way to the apartment, our new home, and the place that we could finally call our own.

Our apartment was located on the first floor of the Cabana Club Towers. We had a one-bedroom, one-bathroom apartment that to us was more than enough room. A routine developed quickly for our lives that consisted of Javier working and me living the life of a stay-at-home mom. I would cook, clean and take care of our son, while Javier would work and make the money to pay the bills. It seemed like it was a simple existence, but for two foreigners who did not speak the language it was a very difficult way to begin our lives. Be that as it may, we made it work.

We also looked into and found out what the requirements were for us, as foreign medical graduates, to be licensed as physicians in the United States. In order to be granted licensing, all we had to do was pass a standardized qualification exam. There were no meetings, there was no need to grease the palm of any politicians, there were no long road trips from city to city, or state to state, only to be shoveled off to another bureaucrat. Nope, the only thing that we were required to do here in the United States was take a test and prove that we were proficient in our craft, and that we possessed the necessary knowledge in order for us to competently practice our profession.

This came as an absolute shock to us, but it also came as a welcome surprise. As a matter of fact, we were even able to take the test right there in Miami. In doing our research into the exam itself, I found one little glitch – in order to successfully pass the exam, you needed to pass two facets of competency. The first I had no fear that both of us could pass with the necessary time to study, but the other facet had me quite worried. You see, in order to pass the ECFMG, which stands for the Educational Commission for Foreign Medical Graduates, you had to pass a medical competency portion of the test. This measures the skills that you should have learned in medical school. We were confident in our training and had no concerns that if we refreshed our skills we would be able to pass this portion of the test. But the second portion was an English skills evaluation. This section measured your command of the English language and your ability to communicate using those language skills. Seeing as I had no language skills, and my husband's were limited, this portion of the test had me more than a little bit concerned.

So there it was. Our gauntlet had been laid, and the obstacle was learning how to speak English effectively enough to pass the test. There were languages classes being offered to foreigners who wanted to learn how to speak English, but those cost money, and we did not have any extra to spend in that way. Besides, we did not know anyone in the area, save for a few friends and neighbors that we met along the way, but there was nobody that we trusted enough to care for our son while we learned the language. Javier was getting good practice at the hospital, and he was becoming more and more effective in his ability to communicate, but I was unable to get the exposure that was required to learn through immersion. That's when I decided I would begin my own immersion technique.

What is the only thing in your home that allows you to hear someone speaking no matter what time of day? That's right, the television! I decided that I would teach myself how to speak English, and my instructor would be the television. There were Spanish-speaking stations at the time in Miami, and they offered entertaining programming, but I knew that if I were to crack the language code, the only way I would be able to do it as a stay-at-home mom, would be to immerse myself in American TV. No, I am not advocating people sitting at home and watching hours upon hours of mindless television, but for my purposes it was the only way I could begin to distinguish between words and try to decipher their meanings. It was a ritual throughout the day as I was minding the house, or taking care of Javier Jr. I would have the television playing in the background. I would watch soap operas and try to follow the plot, which sometimes even if you do speak English is a near impossible feat. If I heard a new word, I would write it down, as best as I could anyway, and try to figure out what it meant.

From the commercials, I gathered enough information to know the names of the household products that we used to clean in the house, as well as the food that we bought on a regular basis. I would write down what we needed, and I would take Javier Jr. to the grocery store to do the shopping. In the beginning, this was about the most frustrating endeavor that anyone could imagine. I would try so hard to pronounce the name of the produce or product correctly, but I just could not get to a point where I was comfortable speaking. So, inevitably, I would be reduced to the status of a child, and I would point and shake if I needed assistance with anything. I cannot tell you how frustrating it was for me to learn a language basically on my own, and how embarrassing it was at times for me. It was a necessity though, and I knew that eventually I would get the hang of it, and I would get the last laugh.

One day, I was flipping through the channels, and I stumbled upon a program that really caught little Javier's attention. It was Sesame Street. Javier Jr. really loved the characters and the music, and basically everything about it. It kept him occupied, and it kept him happy so I left it on. I went back to whatever it was I was doing previously and left my son in front of the television. As I was working around the house, I heard the show in the background, and I heard one of the shows reading segments. I returned to find my son fixated on the screen and found myself becoming fixated on the screen, as well. The characters went through a litany of teaching exercises, and basically had a language and grammar lesson all rolled into one. I sat in a chair next to my son, watching stunned, not ever seeing any sort of show like this before. I sat there for the entirety of the show amazed at how thoroughly they explained all of their lessons, as well as how well the show kept the audience captive. Before I knew it the show was over, and the better part of an hour had passed without me even batting an eye.

"This is great," I thought, "This is the greatest show on television." Not only was it a good teaching tool for my son, but it was also a good teaching tool for me. As such, it became a daily ritual for us. Every day Javier Jr. and I, a son and his mom, would sit in his little chairs both watching the TV and following along with the show, learning English.

Javier Jr. was a smart little boy. There would be times when he would learn the lessons far quicker than I did . He picked the language up faster than anyone could imagine. As a matter of fact, it surprised not only me but my husband, as well. There were times when we would go out on the weekends for some ice cream, or just to do some sightseeing, and Javier Jr. at two years old would walk up to complete strangers and strike up a conversation in English. Then he would come back to us, and seamlessly transfer his conversation and continue speaking to us in Spanish. It was amazing, once that little boy learned how to speak there was nobody in the world, it seemed, that could stop him from saying anything. He was smart, very smart; so smart that at times while we were watching Sesame Street together, and he would understand the lesson before I grasped it, I thought he was a little too smart for his own good, if you know what I mean.

Our lives were going well. We were assimilating well into the community, and aside from the mild embarrassment of not knowing the language well enough to feel comfortable to communicate, we could not complain as to how things were for us. We had our home, Javier had a stable job, and we were both making progress in our studies for the ECFMG. On top of all that, my disease was under control. I had had minor aches and pains continuously since leaving Spain, but I had not experienced any of the violently painful flare-ups that I had suffered through in Europe. I had been on a regimen of mild anti-inflammatory drugs. I would get these as samples mostly, seeing as we could not afford to fill prescriptions at this time, and I was also able to control most of the pains with mild over-the-counter pain relievers, such as Tylenol and Advil.

Time went by, we were happy and things had been going in the right direction for a while for us. We had kept in touch with our families in South America, but we were beginning to come to terms with our new situation, and truth be told we liked our new home. Then we received more great news, I was pregnant again.

The news came as a surprise, but a welcome one at that. We had always planned on expanding our family, but did not think that this great opportunity would come so soon. Javier and I decided that we would not find out the sex of the baby before it was born. The main reason for that was that it cost money to get those scans, and at the time we just did not have the money to pay for such a luxury. Another reason was that we had this romantic notion that the baby would come out as a girl, and, just as we named our first son after my husband, we would name our first daughter after me. She would be Maria Luisa Miller Jr. We convinced ourselves that our second child was destined to be a girl, and any other possibility was just a fleeting thought.

Just like the first time, my pregnancy was phenomenal. For whatever reason, my RA, even though already in check, all but disappeared. I say disappeared in the sense that the pains were few and far between, and they were easily controlled with over-the-counter pain medications. I did not experience any form of morning sickness, and all signs pointed to a healthy baby girl to be added to our growing brood.

Javier continued to work night shift at the hospital, and I continued to study my English and mind the home. We were both focused on passing our test but, with our new addition on the way, we decided to take more family time together and enjoy the beautiful south Florida resources that were free for our enjoyment. We really enjoyed outdoor activities as a family, and we would routinely make the short drive to Key Largo for a family day of fun in the sun. We would lie out on the beach, Javier Jr. would play on the shore, and my husband would fish. It was a great way to entertain ourselves without having to incur any great expense.

As I previously stated, Miami is the first entry port to the United States from South America. It is the quickest large city to get to, and it has a very large Hispanic population. As such, there are a lot of people from Latin American and Caribbean descent who live in the greater Miami area. As is true with any great migration, you get the good with the bad. At the time, Miami was ground zero for the United States' "War on Drugs." Routinely, when we watched the news at night, you would hear the stories of massive drug shipments that were intercepted while being smuggled into the border by air, land or sea. The cocaine shipments that were being brought over from Colombia and South

America were given values into the hundreds of millions of dollars, and those were just the ones that were being intercepted by the police.

Narcotics had grown into a huge business in South Florida, and it had become noticeable. The violence had increased, and insecurity was on the rise. Even with this increase in criminal activity, we still felt safer here than we did in South America. The police here were regulated, and I can safely say the only confrontational contact that I have ever had with government officials in the U.S. has been an officer giving me a traffic ticket. I must admit most of those were deserved, also.

With crime on the rise, and with a small child at home and another on the way, I began to worry about the security that we had at home. This concern evolved particularly because of the erratic nature of my husband's schedule. It was nerve racking when he would have to work nights, and I, a pregnant woman with a small child who did not speak the native language, had to stay at home alone in a city with an increasing drug problem and violence on the rise. I took to strange rituals, and I would disconnect phones prior to going to bed every night when Javier Jr. and I were alone at home. I would disconnect every phone except for the one in the bedroom, for fear of someone breaking in and cutting the line. I would barricade us in our room by locking the doors to every room that could gain access to the bedroom. I was becoming a nervous wreck even though we ourselves had never experienced any sort of crime or violence in the U.S.

As time went by and my pregnancy progressed things continued on the right path for us. On the morning of November 13, 1981, I woke up and immediately knew something was a little off. I called my husband at work and informed him that I thought it was time and the baby was coming. He asked me, "How do you know, are you sure?" I said, "I know because my water broke, and last time I checked we did not have a water bed." He got the picture then and told me to hold tight and pack a bag, he was on his way.

My husband was working the morning shift that day, so he had only been at work for a short while and had to inform his superior that he had to leave immediately because I had gone into labor. Javier was never the type of person to leave work early, ask for multiple days off, or even show up late, so when his boss responded in the way he did it took him completely by surprise. His boss told him that he could not leave, and that if he left he would be fired. Javier sat there for a moment, looked at the man and became irate. He told him that if anything happened to his wife or his child, while he was here arguing with him then his boss would be responsible and he would suffer the consequences. Still the man wouldn't budge. It was almost as if he was trying to say, "I am your boss, and the only reason I am doing this is because I can."

Javier looked him in the eye and said to hell with him. He dropped his things, walked out of the hospital and came home to take me there. Needless to say, when the higher ups at the hospital caught wind of this little exchange, Javier's job was never in any real jeopardy. He came home, and I had packed my little bag to go to the hospital. We took Javier Jr. to a neighbor who we had grown close to, so she could watch him during the delivery, and we started driving to First Baptist Hospital in Miami. My labor pains were minimal, and I told my husband that I was in no rush to get to the hospital, so we took our time on our way and let the moment soak in before our arrival. I add this little quip to emphasize exactly how easy a pregnancy and delivery I had with my second child. It really was enjoyable, as far as pregnancies go.

Once we arrived, we were greeted by the hospital staff in the parking lot. There was a gentleman in a golf cart who saw us driving in. He picked us up at our car to take us to the entrance of the hospital. As we got to the front door of the hospital, the staff was there waiting for us and greeted us with a wheelchair to take me to the delivery room. I looked at the guy with the chair and politely declined the offer. I told him that I thought there were other people in the hospital that may need the chair a little more than I did. It was around nine in the morning, and the doctor, who was going to deliver the baby, had not yet arrived in the hospital. We were led into a patient hospital room, where we were to wait for our doctor.

A few hours went by, and staff members came in and let us know that the doctor was ready and the baby would be delivered. Excitement filled us, as I was led to the delivery room and unabated anticipation filled us, as we could not wait to see our baby girl born. Except there was one problem; we had been so preoccupied that we had not even given any thought to the chance that this baby might be a boy. What would we name him? We had no idea. As I was being carted down the hallway to the delivery room, my husband brought this to my attention, and I remember being somewhat relaxed as I looked up at him, and said, "Well if it is a boy, let's name him Daniel." My husband liked the name, and we agreed that on the off chance that our child, which we knew would be a girl, was indeed born a boy, we would name him Daniel. Although we knew that the chances of this were remote, we were glad that we had given it full consideration, and now we could concentrate on the birth of our daughter.

At 12:45 on November 13, 1981, Daniel Miller was born. What could we say other than "Oops." I guess we were wrong. The day and the delivery had gone by so quickly and relatively painlessly; that we could not believe it was already over. It was less than five hours of labor, and here was our child, our second son. He was a healthy bouncy baby boy, and a big bouncy baby boy at that, weighing in at 9 lbs. 12 oz. I spent the next day in the hospital as the staff made sure that Daniel was healthy and well enough to be released. My husband went to the house to take care of Javier Jr., as they split their time between the hospital and home. Finally, my child and I were released with a clean bill of health. We gathered our things and left the hospital all together as a family for the first time.

We got back to the house, and, for the first time since we had left South America, I realized the true measure of the decision that we had made. On the day I was released from the hospital, there was nobody waiting at home to greet us. There was nobody there to congratulate us on the birth of our son. There was nobody there to volunteer to help us with feedings, or changing, or even to offer support of any kind. When we got back to our house, we returned to an empty house devoid of any family, or friends. On top of that, Javier had to return that night to work, due to the fact that he had already taken the past few days off to tend to me and take care of our son. It was an empty house, but an even emptier feeling upon our return. I felt depressed, I felt sad, and I was overcome with emotion. These feelings did not last long, as I looked down and saw the only two reasons in the world that I needed to understand that the decisions that we made and the actions that we had taken were to make life better for these two little guys sitting at my feet. Things seemed surreal now, and the only people that mattered to us were our kids.

Life went on, and our lives seemed to slip back into a routine that we found comfortable. I continued studying English, but with my new son it was now a three-person class. We finally got to a place where we were comfortable enough in our skills to take the ECFMG exam. As we had thought, the medical portion was difficult, but something that we had considered manageable. The English portion was a whole different story. Because of our elementary knowledge of the language, it took us a few times to pass this portion, but eventually we did. My medical credentials in the United States of America were finally validated. I was now free to pursue my dream of being a pediatrician.

I had decided long before in medical school while doing rotations in my fourth and fifth years that pediatrics was where my heart was. I had seen these children in the hospital so sick and so vulnerable, but they always had this innocence about them. They always wore a smile on their faces, and they always seemed to have a way of putting things in perspective for me. No matter how difficult I thought my day was, or how hard I had things with my disease, I could always find a child whose life had been made infinitely more difficult or sadly shorter, but they still wore a smile. Children are amazingly resilient, and they are remarkably intelligent. They rarely complain, and are always ready with a warm smile, a big hug or that soft look of innocence that just makes you want to help them get better. The first day I walked into my pediatric rotation in Spain while in medical school, I knew that this is why God led me to this calling.

Now that we had our academics in order and our licensing, the next step was to find a job, but you cannot practice medicine in the U.S. until you complete more years of formal training in a hospital setting under the supervision of older more experienced physicians. This period of training is what is called a residency. Residencies are matched through a program of interviews and formal conversations with the heads of hospitals.

We were still a few months off from the interview process commencing, and things were becoming more and more dangerous in South Florida. Crime was still on the rise, and drug abuse seemed to be infecting the entire city. Every news story seemed to begin with a connection to drugs. As I said earlier, we had never experienced any violence or crime in the U.S. ourselves, but that doesn't mean we did not have our close calls. I remember one afternoon being in the apartment alone with my infant son, Danny. My husband had taken Javier Jr. with him to pay an electric bill, and was due to be back relatively quickly. I was tending to the house and my son, when all of the sudden I heard the front door push violently open. I jumped back and screamed terrified by the noise. I looked at the front door and saw an arm reaching in, and I could hear a woman's voice screaming, "Let me in woman; let me in." I saw that the chain on the door was the only thing separating me from this enraged person. I had no idea who she was, or what she wanted. I quickly grabbed my child, as I could see her fighting with the chain and screaming at the top of her lungs. I raced to the back window and opened it. I started climbing out, as I could hear her getting closer and closer to breaking the chain off the door, and I was having difficulty getting myself into a position with a child in my arms to safely climb out of the window. My adrenaline was pumping, and fear was gripping me, clouding my mind and fighting against me. I was terrified, and I could not process my actions, I finally looked up and saw my husband and my son, as I was halfway out of the window, and screamed his name. He saw me and began running. I yelled, "There's someone at the door, there's someone trying to break in at the door." He ran to my aid, but by the time he got to the front door she was gone.

My husband saw the woman running down the hall and escaping into an elevator. We later found out that she was an employee of the building who had a serious drug addiction. She was fired for her actions that day, but the incident served to instill a fear in me that I would carry forever. I was so scared that I convinced my husband that we needed a gun. He understood my fears and relented. We bought a handgun and received shooting lessons at the Tamiami gun range. My fears were still not put to rest, though. For quite some time, I carried a knife with me underneath my son's stroller for fear that this woman, who had lost her job because of me, would seek retribution. She knew where I lived, she knew for the most part our schedule, and she was a confirmed drug addict. I was not proud of my actions, but I would do anything to protect my kids, and I would be damned if some woman who had made bad decisions in her own life was going to affect mine.

After a while, we realized that it would probably be best if we moved to a different place, somewhere new for a fresh start. We had saved up enough money to put a down payment on a place of our own, so we decided to upgrade apartments. We moved into an apartment in Kendal near Miami, which was the first place that we could truly call our own. This move was short lived, as soon thereafter the residency-matching program began, and as it is a nationwide match we did not know exactly where we would end up.

We had both set our sights on hospitals in South Florida to continue our training, but life sometimes has a way of throwing curve balls at you. It turned out that after all of our interviews and explaining to everyone our unique situation with our boys being so young, my husband matched for a program in South Florida, and, of all places, I matched for a pediatric residency in New York City. As the saying goes, life has a way of going full circle, and here I was. Just a few years after landing in New York City as a pit stop for our life in South America, I was now in a position where I would be living there on a more permanent basis.

There was one big problem, though. My husband had matched in South Florida. We were a young married couple, we had two very young children, and now we were being asked to separate the family and train on opposite ends of the east coast. This was not an option. We were unable to convince the powers that be to find me a position in South Florida, so my husband sacrificed, and we did the only thing we could. We packed up our home, our little boys, and whatever belongings we had and drove up the east coast to our new home of New York City.

We were going blind: no home, no family, save for an aunt of my husband, and no knowledge of the city that we would now call ours. My husband did not have a position to continue his training, but we did what we had to do, and we left Miami in 1983 to pursue our American dream.

CHAPTER 5

*"Experience: that most brutal of teachers.
But you learn, my God do you learn."*
—*C.S. LEWIS*

Of all places, New York City was to be our new home for the next foreseeable portion of our lives. How did this come to pass? I feel as though the explanation deserves a more detailed and thorough explanation, rather than just matching for a residency and off we were. While living in Miami and being blessed enough to be able to earn our way into the credentialed world of physicians in this great country, we were basically left stranded. You see, everything for us was new and foreign, not just the land and the language, but also the procedures and the competition of our new capitalist home. Physicians in the U.S. are some of the greatest in the world, and the medical programs are also graduating some extremely qualified doctors on a yearly basis. This is not to say that we were not just as qualified, but in all reality we were at a severe disadvantage. We did not speak the language as well as the others, and we had a family to consider at home.

Although I do not believe that having children should be looked upon negatively in the least bit, in the early 1980s things were not as politically correct as they are now. So, imagine me walking into meetings in hospitals with these high-level executives, and attempting to market myself as their next great physician in training. The cards were stacked against me. Not only did I speak relatively little English still, but I had my boys at home and my husband was also a physician seeking a residency position.

In those days, the hours that were requested of resident physicians were ghastly. We would work 100-hour weeks without blinking an eye. We would be driven to the point of exhaustion, only to be told to come back in a few hours, because you had to do it all over again. I knew this and my husband knew it as well, but we would not be denied. We had come too far to be stopped when it was so close to our reach.

I had some relatively constructive meetings with hospitals in and around the South Florida area, and I had interviews granted in New York, as well. The process was long and difficult for me; I was beginning to grow frustrated in my interviews, as I was unable to completely express myself and my desire, due to the language barrier. It all came to a head one day in Jacksonville, Florida.

I had been granted an interview in one of the area hospitals for a pediatric residency position. I was thrilled, and was looking forward to the opportunity to gain a position in the state of Florida. I was even more thrilled to learn that I would be interviewing with a gentleman who himself was a foreign medical graduate. He was the head of the pediatric unit in this particular hospital, and he was a graduate of a medical school somewhere in Southeast Asia. He had been in the country for over 20 years, and he had ascended to a position that one day I wanted to be in. I thought if anyone knows the path that we have taken and would likely be sympathetic to our cause, it would be this gentleman. I thought I had lucked out. I thought this was the greatest opportunity that we could have ever asked for, and we were destined to remain in Florida.

I arrived in Jacksonville excited and thrilled to be in the position that I was. I was prepared, I was going to wow them, and I was going to earn that position that day.

I entered the hospital with my head held high. I was on cloud nine, and nobody was going to knock me off this pedestal. I was confident, I was collected, and I had practiced all of the tough questions that I thought could possibly be asked of me. I arrived in this gentleman's office and was greeted by his assistant. Everyone thus far had been polite and welcoming. I was confident, I was ready. After a few minutes, the assistant led me into the interview room, and there he was – the man who just a few short years ago was in the same position that I was in, a man who knew exactly how I felt in this moment of time in my life. I thought we shared common ground, and he would be receptive to what I had to say. I extended my hand to introduce myself in a firm and confident way to let him know, "I am serious, and I want this more than any other candidate that you have seen in your time here." I said, "Hello, I am Dr. Maria Miller." He greeted me, and gestured for me to sit down. Immediately, I knew something was off; there was tension in the air; there was something wrong.

He sat in his chair for a moment and looked at me for an extended period of time. Then he looked down at his folder. He reached over, picked his folder up and read the jacket. He looked over the top of the jacket at me, and asked, "Are you Maria Miller?" I said, "Yes, I am Dr. Maria Miller." He leaned back and stared. I asked, "Is everything all right?" He replied, "Everything is fine, only that it is very difficult to understand you, you have a very thick accent." I was devastated, but he did not stop there. He then went on to say, "How do you expect to work in a hospital if you can't even understand the people around you, and they can't understand you?" I felt like crying. I felt as though all of the hard work that I had put in, all of the time that I had invested in learning the language, as well as studying to prove that I was deserving of my position in this country as a physician that was earned not entitled, had been destroyed in a five-minute greeting.

The interview continued, but it was painfully obvious that this gentleman was not interested. I kept my composure and thanked him for the opportunity for the position. He was dismissive, and ushered me to the door and out of his program. Outside I felt like crying, I felt like breaking down, and I almost felt for the first time like throwing in the towel. Then anger began to take hold of me. I began to think, "Who is this guy to question my work ethic? Who is this guy to question my desire and my dreams?" I began to calm myself, and then I even started to amuse myself with the thoughts racing through my mind. Some were very comical, such as, "This guy has been in the country for over 20 years, and his accent is almost as thick as mine." It began to amaze me how people's initial reactions are to destroy and degrade rather than help one another to achieve shared goals.

I put this experience behind me and became even more determined to match in a program that not only I cared for, but also cared for me. I needed to be around people who wanted to help me succeed in order for me to be able to achieve my best for them, as well. I found this in New York City, specifically in Flushing Meadows Hospital in Queens, New York.

Now that I knew where I would be working, I had to confront an issue that I had never even dreamed of tackling at this stage in my life. My husband and I knew that we were moving to New York City, and we knew that our work schedules would be completely opposite from each other, and chances were that we would not even be working in the same hospital. Problem: I didn't know how to drive. Not only did I not know how to drive, I had never been behind the wheel of a car in my life, let alone driven one. Now I was facing the reality of having to drive in New York, one of if not the most hectic and unrelenting cities in the world. What was I going to do?

The mission was at hand, and my husband took the challenge like a champion. He knew it would not be easy, and it would not be fast, but he took the initiative and decided to teach me how to drive a car. We began our lessons in the parking lot of our apartment in Kendal. Surprisingly things went well. I got the hang of driving with minimal incident and minimal mishaps. I say minimal, because there was one little tiny incident that occurred in the early goings of my tutelage.

We were practicing my close-quarters maneuvering in the parking lot of our apartment, when I attempted to try my hand at narrow-space parking for the first time. I had picked out a spot that I thought might be reflective of the type of parking situations I would face in a big city like New York, and made my decision to try and conquer this vital driving skill. I made my approach listening to my husband/instructor, and following all of his advice. As I made my way towards the parking spot, I made an error in my perception and without warning we heard a noise that we did not want to hear. We heard a God-awful sound of metal on metal screeching. We immediately jumped out of the car assessed the damage, and did what anybody would do. We parked the car as far away from the spot of the accident as possible, and ran like hell back to our apartment.

Now I'm not condoning this type of behavior, but what were we going to do? We were young, we didn't have any money, and we thought we were going to get away with it. We almost did, too – almost! The rest of that day went by without word of the incident, and at the time of the accident the parking lot was empty. Or so we thought. That next morning, we got a knock on our door. We were seated around the breakfast table, a rare weekend breakfast that we could all enjoy together, when we heard the loud rap. My husband answered the door, and I could not really hear the conversation, but I knew by his body language that it was not anything too serious. He spoke with the person for a few seconds, and then returned to the table no worse for wear. I asked him who that was at the door, and he just looked at me and cracked a smile. "Oh that was just the guy who owns the car that you hit yesterday." "What?" I screamed. He laughed and did his best to calm me down. "It's OK," he said, "The guy only wants us to pay for the paint, he's not even that mad." It's funny the things that run through your mind when you get caught doing something bad. It's almost like you revert to being a child, where you try to cover yourself by deflecting blame. The only thing that I could think to say was, "I didn't think anyone saw us." We had a good laugh about it, and we obviously paid the kind man for the damage to his car. If he reads this, I just want to say I'm sorry for scratching up your car. That may be too little too late, but what else can I say? I still wonder how he found out it was us that hit his car. I could have sworn there was nobody else in that parking lot.

All these incidents help to explain why we began our adventure of getting to New York, but now we were on our way with no real plan, other than me knowing that soon after we arrived I had to report for work at the hospital. Everything else surrounding our lives was literally up in the air.

The first order of business, once we arrived in the city, was to find a place to live. We found a nice little brownstone in a complex of row houses in Jamaica Hills, Queens. It abutted Grand Central Parkway, which gave it great access to major roadways, and was literally only minutes away from the hospital. We thought that this would be a good location for us to live, since it was close enough to work that if anything happened I could easily come home to deal with it, but also it gave us the room that we needed for our family.

Once we arrived, the second order of business was for Javier to find a program so that he would be able to continue his medical training. Luckily we were given some good advice from colleagues, and he was pointed in the right direction when he, too, was offered a pediatric residency position at Lincoln Memorial Hospital in New York City. We were all set to begin work and settle into our new life as resident physicians in the United States. Then something else dawned on us.

We were going to be asked to work 100-hour weeks, and at times these shifts were going to overlap. We had a four-year-old son, who was about to begin school and we had one-and-a-half-year-old son, who needed constant vigilance and care. We began to wonder, and even doubt whether or not we had made the right choice. How were we going to raise our two children, two very young children, and be able to work the kind of hours demanded of resident training physicians? This was a problem that arose unexpectedly in the midst of all of the excitement of interviewing and progressing towards our ultimate goal.

We did not know what to do, and we did not know where to turn. Javier had an aunt who lived in New York, but she was already in her late 60s and would not be able to give the type of care to the boys that they needed. Not that she would not have gladly done it, because she was and still is a wonderful lady, but you have to understand my sons were a handful at this young age. They had more energy than a group of 10 children, and it was a job in itself trying to keep tabs on them and make sure they were staying out of trouble. At that age, kids are curious by nature, and to trouble someone with that type of burden on a regular basis, I felt would be unfair.

At this point, we sat down and had an in-depth conversation as to exactly what we needed to do. As we saw it, we only had two choices. The first was to put the kids in daycare, which we never wanted to do. The reasons for that were twofold. First, I just never wanted strangers to take care of my kids. Not that there is anything wrong with daycare, but I just never felt comfortable with that scenario. Second, daycare was expensive, and we just did not have the money for it. We had just moved, we had just rented a house, and we had just bought a new car for me to get to and from work. Money was tight. It was flowing out, and at this point we did not have very much flowing in. Daycare was not a realistic option for us. The other idea was for one of us to forego our residency, and maybe attempt to qualify later for a program. This option would then allow that person to be the full-time caretaker of the kids and assume the role of primary caregiver for the kids.

This option was valid, and it seemed the most plausible and realistically the most reasonable course of action for us to take. I mean, it gave us the ability to save money, as well as guaranteeing us the peace of mind that our kids would be cared for in the way in which they had grown accustomed. Javier Jr. would be starting school soon, and Danny was always a really easy baby to care for. If either of us could wait a year or so, things at home would be much easier to adapt to in that time frame.

For all of the rationalizing and all of the convincing that we did with ourselves, this option just did not seem right. We had traveled all of this distance from Miami to New York for this purpose. It was for the betterment of not only our lives, but also for the lives of our boys. We had overcome so many obstacles, to be placed in a position where we could now both succeed. To be placed in this position at this point where we were so close to achieving our dreams was difficult, but at this time our decisions could not be made based upon what we felt was best for us. We had to think of the boys, and we had to make a decision based on what was best for them. With this in mind, the decision did not seem so difficult. We would do anything for them, and if delaying the start of our programs a little bit was the best course of action, then so be it.

We had almost resigned ourselves to this option where one of us would forego the beginning of our training, when Javier had another idea as to how we may be able to make things work. He suggested that we could possibly hire his sister, Victoria, as a nanny for the boys to care for them while we worked our hospital shifts, and she could live with us in our house rent-free as partial payment. She could also pursue any type of schooling or job opportunities in New York that she would want, as she was young, single and in a position to explore new opportunities in the most thriving metropolitan city in the world.

We approached her with our proposal, and we laid everything on the table. We made ourselves vulnerable and told her exactly how difficult a situation we were in. We also told her that we knew we were putting her in a difficult situation, moving to a new country, as she was still living in Colombia, but we also tried to express all of the benefits that the city had to offer. After a little coaxing and some in-depth discussions, she agreed to move to New York to help care for the kids while we needed her and while we began our career journey.

It was one of those things that you almost feel is a certainty, but when so many minor stumbling blocks keep presenting themselves, you begin to doubt yourself. For us, we did not know when or where, or even if we would be able to do what it was that we felt we were put on this earth to do. To realize that for which we had studied so hard, and fought so long to achieve, was fulfilling. We had persevered though all of our struggles and finally had the chance to attain the opportunity that we had sought for so long. Everything was in place, and we were ready to begin working in the United States of America as medical doctors.

My first day at work as a pediatric resident was an amazing experience that I will never forget. I was very nervous and the low man on the totem pole, as they say, and already I had some feelings of uncertainty due to the fact that I knew absolutely nobody at this hospital, and I still had a little bit of trouble fully expressing myself in the English language. After I arrived in the afternoon for the night shift, I was told that the only three people on staff for the evening in the hospital were me and two other residents. I was terrified. My first day of work in a major New York City hospital, I along with two other residents was in charge of caring for all of the patients on the pediatric floor, as well as covering the entire emergency room. Needless to say, it was a baptism by fire, but I was also flattered at the confidence that they displayed in me. I took pride in the fact that they trusted me enough to place me in that type of intense situation, but I was not prepared for the nerves that would engulf me that night.

A pediatric floor in a hospital is typically a calm and orderly place, but when the reality hits you that you are ultimately in charge of what happens with regards to the care of these sick kids, it becomes an awesome responsibility, and one for which I'm not so sure that I was fully prepared. The kids on the floor were stable and on the mend, but there was that always ever-present chance that something could go wrong. Things could and had gone very wrong in seemingly the most innocuous of times, but thankfully that night nothing happened, and I was able to count myself lucky that I survived the first of what would certainly be many sleepless and nerve-racking evenings.

This time in my life was marked by many landmarks. First, we moved to the most thriving metropolis in the world; then, we secured positions as training physicians in competitive learning hospitals in one of the busiest, fast-paced health communities in the world. The next step was our oldest son, Javier, needed to start school.

Up to this point, this moment had seemed so far away. I mean, it seemed like only yesterday that Javier Jr. was born, and we were living in Spain. Four short, and I do mean extremely short, years had gone by already. We had already experienced so much in that span, but now we were facing the tough reality that our sons were growing up, and growing up fast before our eyes. The public school system in New York was good, but the area we lived in, and the stories that we had heard of the schools, had us afraid to enroll Javier in that system.

We searched the city and tried to receive input from colleagues and friends that we had met in the city regarding education. The consensus came back that private school was the way to go. Seeing as how we did not know much about the school system, and how things worked regarding education in this country, we took their word for it. We set off looking for a good school close to home in which we could enroll Javier Jr. We ended up finding a Catholic school in Queens, that was a short, 10-minute walk from the house and that we felt was on par with our idea of a proper education. The school was run by nuns and had been given good reviews by those people that we had asked. There was a church attached that we had sort of adopted as our home parish, and the teachers and staff seemed sincere. Another unexpected problem that arose from this search was the realization that we now had to budget for private school tuition. This played a major role in our decision-making process, but in the end the benefits and peace of mind knowing that we were comfortable in a Catholic setting, like the one we had experienced as kids, was worth the extra price. Don't get me wrong, we had to make adjustments and sacrifice some small creature comforts to afford private school tuition, but in the end it was the best decision for us.

Time was flying by for us in New York, as work was grueling. Grueling may even be an understatement because the hours required of us were exhausting, and at times you wondered if the effort was worth it. I had begun to feel as though my life at home might be suffering. I mean with my oldest just starting school and my youngest son still only at the toddler stage, it was very difficult for my husband and me to justify to ourselves the long hours that we were both away from them. In the long run, we knew that doing this now was providing for a better future for them later. No matter how much you justify, or how many excuses you create in your mind, it is still easy for a parent to feel as though they are trapped in a puzzle where they feel as though work may be taking away from family. In the long run, it is obvious that the choices we made then and the plan we followed was the best for us and our sons; and those choices were made easier by being able to have my sister-in-law at the house, helping care for the kids. She was family, and we knew that we could trust the care she was giving the boys.

For about the first year, we took our time to settle into our routine and settle into it we did. I was able to get into a groove at work learning my craft, and I was becoming ever more confident in my abilities as a doctor. I loved seeing sick kids and being part of their road to recovery, and I was becoming ever more confident in my abilities with the language. Similarly for my husband, work was progressing, and we felt that we kept a healthy balance between home life and work life as best we could.

Since arriving in the country, my illness had been kept well under control for the most part. I had not had any of the serious flare ups that I had last experienced in Spain, and, with the low dosage of medication and a regimen of over-the-counter pain relievers, I had been fairly successful at diminishing, if not almost eliminating, the pain. I had come to a comfortable place in dealing with my disease, and realized that although not the most ideal of situations, there were many people in the world that were affected much, much worse than I was. If I could maintain the disease at its current levels, then I believed I had conquered what had been described to me at my initial consultation in Spain as a debilitating and crushing disease.

However, during my second year in New York, things took a drastic turn for what I believed to be the worse. As I have previously described, RA is a debilitating disease in its inner aspect, causing unbelievable pain and agony. The swelling and stiffness to the sufferer's body are of the type to which only a person with the disease could imagine or relate. The other painful aspect is the mental pain that suffers experience with this disease. With RA, there is associated depression and anxiety for people. I had never really experienced this aspect of the disease in the past, as I had focused all of my energies in curing the pain and moving on. It was always an attempt to eliminate the pain and continue with my life. Sure I had rough days where the pain seemed unbearable, but those days had never risen to the level where it affected my mood tremendously or what I would consider depression or anxiety.

During my second year in New York that all changed. RA can cause what so-called experts deem to be deformities in the person carrying the diseased body. I never liked the term deformities, and I still don't like the word deformities, and since it is my book I will not use it. That being said, the disease causes certain physical changes in a person's body. I had not yet experienced any permanent physical changes due to my disease. I had been lucky in that respect, but I still did not have too much knowledge with regard to the disease itself. So, as time flew by, and as we were immersing ourselves in our new roles in this wonderful country, certain changes in my body began to take place. The pains had returned, but not to the point where it was intolerable. To be quite honest with you, during residency there are not very many times where your health takes precedence over the health of others. The changes began subtly, but they were noticeable.

First, my hands became stiffer and stiffer. It became increasingly difficult to straighten my fingers, and bend them so as to ball my hands into a fist. Over time, the stiffness became more permanent. I was progressively losing the ability to manipulate my hands in the way that I had always been accustomed to doing. Gradually the stiffness turned permanent, and my hands began to take a different shape. The ultimate result of this change is what is known as a swan-neck "deformity," again that word that I refuse to utter other than in clinical description. This type of change is called this because of its literal appearance. Although difficult to imagine, I will do my best to explain exactly what it means, so as to paint a broader picture of the situation.

In this type of physical change, the fingers on both hands become straightened to a point where the four fingers, for the most part, are permanently in a pointed position. It is very difficult to bend the fingers, and nearly impossible to ball them. The knuckles of the hand swell, as well. Due to the damage and the repeated trauma caused by the disease, the bones in the knuckles begin to take a permanently different shape. The growth is exaggerated and the hand takes on a fixed, bent appearance. This is exactly what was happening to me. This process happens over time, and in all reality the damage never ceases, it continues, and the joint continues to suffer damage as long as the symptom remains untreated. The reason it is called swan neck is because the resulting formation of the hand literally resembles the neck of a swan, with a protruding lump near the knuckles and stiff, straight fingers pointed outward. I was now beginning to suffer the outward symptoms of my disease.

It began to take a mental toll on me. I had never been, and still to this day have never been one to ask for pity or sympathy from anyone. I do not want people to feel bad for me, or sorry for me. I do not take well to people's charity towards me for sympathy's sake. I refuse to be a victim, and this feeling has always been ingrained in me. This time in my life was no different. On the other hand, I had never faced a challenge like this in my life. For all of the ups and downs that I had faced thus far in my life, they were from choices that I had made, and the consequences I readily accepted. This was a whole different animal, I did not choose this disease, and I certainly did not want to deal with these physical changes that I was experiencing. It was shocking, and it was troubling, and I did not know how to handle it.

After initially experiencing the swan-neck condition in my hands, other outward physical changes began to take hold. I began to experience foot and knee pains in both legs. My joints began to ache more and more, and as a result I began to suffer similar deformities in my feet, as I was experiencing in my hands. I felt helpless, and to an extent I began to question what I had done to deserve such an awful, awful fate. The changes did not end there; after some time, the aches began to travel up into my elbows, and soon enough it felt like every single joint in my body was relentlessly sobbing and begging me for the mercy of pain relief. I developed rheumatoid nodules in my elbows at this point in time, as well.

I had begun an entire transformation from the person I was to this new person that I had become. As women, we are predisposed or conditioned to care about our aesthetic, outward appearance. I don't know why that is, but I feel as though we want to look good, and we take pride in ourselves. These transformations were devastating to me. I did everything in my power to hide them and cover up any changes, because to me they were a source of weakness and embarrassment. I now knew what was meant by the psychological pain that this disease brought to its sufferers.

In the beginning, I avoided any and all situations where I would have to show my hands. You would regularly see me with my arms crossed or folded in front of me so that my hands would be hidden from sight. I would wear long sleeves to cover my arms, so that nobody could notice my elbows or swollen wrists and knuckles. During leisure time, I would make every excuse to wear closed-toe shoes so that nobody could see my toes, and the effects that the disease was having on my feet. It was a conscious effort daily to hide myself and shun people's attention from what I perceived as an embarrassing sickness. I blamed myself mostly, and this began to take a mental toll on my psyche. I began to feel helpless, even trapped in my own body. Not only was I dealing with the daily pain associated with this disease, but now I also had to deal with the changes to my physical appearance. It was grueling mentally. I began to experience depression for the first time. I began to ask myself questions that I never thought I would ask. I wondered if I deserved this, or if I had angered God in some way, and this was my punishment. Was I destined to be this way and, worse yet, were there more changes in store?

Not only was my appearance and mood altered, but physically my capabilities became limited, as well. When the physical changes began to take shape my sons were still very young. I found it difficult to do the things that I had grown accustomed to doing with them in Miami. Playing with them became difficult due to the fact that I had not grown used to the limitations I was experiencing with my hands. I could not play catch or basketball with them, and I could not run and play tag with them like I wanted. One of the most difficult things, both emotionally and mentally, that I had dealt with was admitting this to myself. I would find myself making excuses to my little boys as to why their mommy could not play with them. I did not know what they thought. They could have thought I just did not want to play, or I was busy with something else, but one thing for sure was that they could not have understood that mommy was unable to play because she was experiencing excruciating pain and to play with them meant causing even greater unbearable pain. One thing I was not willing to do was to look into those little innocent eyes and for any reason at all have them feel as though they had any hand or responsibility in why their mom was hurt. So what did I do? I did everything in my power to cover up the fact that I felt any pain related to my disease. As a matter of fact, I did everything in my power to cover up the fact that there was anything wrong with me at all. I denied having any disease, and I made excuses as to why I would not place myself in situations that I knew would be painful, or too difficult for me to withstand.

We had made friends in New York, and one friend, in particular, had boys who were a few years older than my boys. A prime example of the lengths I would go to in order to cover my pain was a day, like any other, when I had been feeling the daily aches and pains associated with the disease.

My friend had invited me and my boys to join her and her children in the park for an afternoon of outdoor fun. We joined them and enjoyed our afternoon. During our time there, we had a scenario where everyone was seated in a circle having a few laughs and generally having a good time. To anyone else, this may seem to be an innocuous if not harmless everyday routine. I mean, sitting on the floor and exchanging fun and conversation with friends is commonplace for most of us. Unfortunately for someone who suffers from RA this can be one of the most difficult and stress-inducing scenarios imaginable. The effort it would have taken for me to sit down on the pavement next to my children and play would have been extreme. Not to mention that, with the condition that my hands and feet were in, I did not feel as though I possessed the stability to avoid injury or incident. I could not withstand the embarrassment if I were to fall or hurt myself in front of my kids. This was my thought process for sitting down only. Now imagine, if I were to successfully sit down. If I had conquered that maneuver, I would have to stay in a seated position for an extended period of time, and then when everyone else easily just stood up, I would have to fight my way back to my feet. I would have to straighten stiff legs, endure the pain of swollen knees and feet. I would then have to find a way to support my weight as I struggled to my feet, and then attempt to maintain my balance all the while avoiding taking a catastrophic tumble before my very own children's eyes due to weakness in my back and legs.

This was my dilemma: a simple maneuver, such as sitting down in a park with my kids, had become a deliberate process that involved many intricate levels of thought. I decided against sitting down and opted to stand. There I was standing over my group in the park looking as awkward as can be looming over my children, who repeatedly asked their mom to sit. It was difficult to tell them, "No, mommy just wants to stand," and after a while the repetition to them might have seemed to give off a tone of anger and annoyance. This was not my intent. The irritation in my voice was a reflection of my despair and frustration towards my inability to interact with my children in the way that I wanted to. It was annoyance, but annoyance that stemmed from inside, not from these two poor little children who only wanted to play with their mom. Unfortunately, people cannot see what is going on in someone else's mind, and irritation is usually perceived as annoyance with others. This was my new reality, a reality filled with simple decisions made complicated due to the unforeseen effects of a debilitating disease.

For the most part, while we lived in New York I felt as though I covered my disease well. I had done my best to keep the physical changes from prying eyes as best as I could, and I thought I had done a relatively good job. I was dead wrong. As time progressed in the hospital, it became more and more difficult for me to find ways to hide my hands. As a physician, or even just as a functioning member of society, you use your hands on a daily basis. That is just how things work. In addition to one's mouth, your hands are front and center in your daily life as tools, and vehicles of work and communication. This is ever so true in the medical field. It is very difficult to perform a physical, or check someone's lungs without exposing your hands. If we break it down to its most simplistic roots, a person, not a physician, but anybody in daily greetings or formal introductions usually shakes hands or gives a wave to say hello. People are not really that aware of how much we use our hands in our everyday routine, until that point in time where they consciously try to hide them from society.

I had lived that way for quite sometime, as I have previously stated, trying to hide my hands from society. This was a difficult, if not impossible, task. After a while, people began to notice my physical appearance. They began to comment on my hands and how they looked. They would ask questions and attempt to elicit explanations as to why they looked the way they did.

I do not know if it was out of frustration, or embarrassment, or possibly even personal denial, but I would make excuse after excuse as to why my hands looked like they did. I would give every excuse imaginable except for the truth. I never wanted to admit that the reason my hands had the form that they did was because I suffered from RA. My favorite excuse went something like this: In an ever so common exchange after a colleague or patient asked what was wrong with my hands, and yes people were so dense then to take that rough and crass approach, I looked at them pensively. I asked them what they meant what was wrong with my hands? They would usually repeat the question, and ask why they looked the way that they did. I then responded that when I was a child I had suffered some sort of riding or farm accident, and I had broken both hands. I told them that during the healing process this was how the bones healed. I assured them that nothing was wrong with my hands; they were still fully functional, which I would demonstrate by grasping a pen and writing, and, in a dismissive tone, I said that everything was just fine.

Here I was, a doctor telling other doctors who presumably had the same level of training as I did that the gradual changes in my hands and the swelling in my joints was due to a childhood fracture in my bones. It was a stretch, and it was a bad lie, but people would accept it and walk away. I do not know if they believed it, or if they just felt pity for their newfound knowledge that I could not accept the fact that I was uncomfortable with how my body looked due to this disease. Rest assured, I was uncomfortable with these changes. I found it embarrassing, and I looked for every excuse in the world to try to skirt the topic.

You learn a lot about the character of others, as well as the character of yourself when you experience something like this. In a sense it was a transformation for me, both internally and externally. There were people who never even brought the topic of my disease or my appearance up in conversation. These were the friends that I began to feel most comfortable around. They knew that there was something different about my appearance, and those who were doctors knew exactly what was wrong, but they looked passed it. They saw me for the person inside, and never questioned me or brought up my disease. Then there were others. They had to know everything and were filled with hundreds of questions, questions that frankly I did not feel I had a duty to answer to anyone.

New York was a tough time in my life and for my family. It was a time of realization and epiphany for me. Through our time in South America and Florida, my disease was what I would have considered to be under control and all but eliminated. Prior to our move, I thought I had finally conquered this disease. When my physical changes began to occur, and the disease began to take a whole other psychological dimension, I was not prepared or expecting it. It was a revelation, and I was smacked square across the face with it.

I retreated inwards. I began to avoid public situations, and I tried to hide myself and bury myself with my kids and my home life. I would only feel comfortable going out publicly to go to work, and I would avoid public functions because I did not want to deal with what I perceived would be a relentless and endless stream of questions and critiques. I did not have many friends, and I kept it that way on purpose. I figured the fewer people around me, the less people needed explanations. It was a time of awakening and a time where I really struggled to find comfort and peace with who I truly was.

This is not to say that all the times were bad in New York, and that I was relegated to the status of a hermit, holed up in our house and only seeing the light of day when I went to work. We were lucky enough to have some truly great friends in New York and some truly great neighbors. Javier's aunt lived in New York, and having her there really helped us assimilate to our new surroundings, but she lived in a different neighborhood. Luckily we had the good fortune of moving into a home next door to a friendly older couple, Ruth and Marcel, who always went out of their way to make sure that we and the boys were doing all right. They were a retired couple, in their late 60s or early 70s who still remained active. On countless times we would see them in their backyard or their porch, and every time I, my husband, or the boys would be greeted with a warm smile, or some form of homely greeting.

On the other side of our house lived Carlos and Natchita, a Peruvian couple who also had two kids. They were a little older than Javier and me, but not much, and they, too, were so caring and so helpful at every turn. It was a small thing, but a really important one when moving to a strange town to be able to develop that feeling of home, and our neighbors really did that for us. Knowing that we had people we could rely on really made our transition to New York that much easier. Along the way other people came into our lives, but for the most part they were passing acquaintances. That was fine with me, because I was just at a place in my life where I felt as though everybody was analyzing me like I was some sort of science experiment.

There was one couple that we met that to this day my husband and I consider to be our closest friends. I won't get into the details of it, but when people talk about good, honest and loyal people, they are the epitome of that. The husband was a doctor who worked with my husband in Lincoln hospital. He and his wife were from the Dominican Republic. He had been in the country a little bit longer than us, and he and Javier immediately got off on the right foot. They became close at work which, in turn, led to the families becoming close in our personal lives. They had a son, who was the same age as Javier Jr., and a daughter who was a few years older than him. The kids got along great, and we did, too. We got along so well that we began taking vacations and family trips together on a consistent basis. This provided a great escape for me, as well. It was a time when I knew I could be myself surrounded by family, and not need to worry about people asking me questions about my hands and my disease.

We did everything together, we would plan skiing trips with them, and we even made our first significant luxury purchase together. They told us of this beautiful region in the mountains of Pennsylvania that they would frequently visit all year around. We planned a trip with them one weekend during the summer and fell in love with the place. We ended up buying a week in a timeshare plan at a cabin in the woods of Pocono Mountain, which we still use as a family to this day.

I guess the point that I am trying to make is that, with all of the changes and what I perceived to be terrible things happening within my body at that time, it could have been very easy for me to give up. I was lucky that, to some degree, I surrounded myself with people who would not let me give up. There was always a positive attitude. Even though at times I felt as though I was in the depths of despair with pain and suffering as a result of my disease, I always knew there was a light at the end of the tunnel. It could have been a tiny flicker, or a speck in the far distance, but there was definitely a light always on the horizon.

Because of my inner struggles and my discomfort with my outward appearance, I did not meet or allow myself to get to know many people that I should have. Some people could have provided invaluable life experiences, and some others may have just been there for casual conversations. The bottom line is that I would not allow myself this luxury. There was one place where I knew that I would never be a stranger, and certain people I knew would never and could never pass judgment on me, my family. I never felt as though my boys had ever looked at me differently or wondered about my health. I never felt the stinging feeling of pity or empathy that I so despise come from their little innocent eyes. It was always just the opposite. They always looked to my husband and me for protection and guidance. These two little guys never saw anything in me other than their mom, and that was a feeling of normalcy that I desired to always feel. In front of them and at home I never had to pretend, I never had to hide or act as though there was something wrong with me that needed to be covered up. It was a feeling of security and a feeling that I craved. So, I immersed myself in that world, and I embraced it for what it was – a comfort zone where I could control the environment and know that nobody would be passing judgment over me.

My husband, as well, provided a sense of comfort. He had been with me from the beginning of my journey with this disease. We had walked through this journey together, and he had never passed judgment. He helped me in Spain when I was initially diagnosed, and throughout our time as students and throughout our marriage he had always been a partner who helped try to find the remedy to the unbearable pain that I felt. There was never a feeling of condescension, quite the opposite. He never pretended to know how bad the pains from this disease were, he was just there to help try to alleviate them. We had gone through great lengths in trying to resolve my issues, and those adventures had brought us closer together. When my physical changes began to take hold, we did not know what to make of them. Still, I never felt as though in his eyes there was anything wrong with me. I never felt a sense of pity, and I never felt a sense of sympathy from him. He knew the disease, but he looked past it and saw his wife. This added to my sense of comfort at home. I was happy there, and it was the place where I felt I truly belonged.

I say that I felt like this only at home with one caveat. At work, I met this wonderful doctor by the name of Dr. Phyllis Wiener. Dr. Wiener was the emergency room director of Flushing Hospital. Dr. Wiener was not only the ER director; she was also the head of the Child Protection Team for the entire borough of Queens. As I was a pediatric resident under the supervision of Dr. Wiener, I had a lot of contact with her, as well as a lot of exposure to the child-abuse victims that came through the hospital.

For the most part the job was satisfying and even gratifying, save for the times when the serious abuse victims would come into the hospital. There were some serious and heartbreaking cases of abuse that we would see on a regular basis. It was an honor working on these cases, as we got to help and nurture these children back to health, but it was also agonizing to know that, once these poor children were released, the only thing they had to look forward to or the only home they knew would be filled with the same anger, rage and abuse that brought them to our care in the first place.

Witnessing this abuse gave me a great perspective on life. I had two boys of my own at home, and to see children suffer like this gave me great pause for reflection. I reflected on my family, and wondered how someone could do these monstrous things to a child. I would die for my kids, just to protect them from any sort of harm. How could some demon hurt a poor innocent child the way that these poor children were brutalized at the hands of the very people that were charged with protecting them? I could not wrap my head around this, and I could not understand the nonsensical behavior that some adults engaged in to simply destroy something as beautiful and innocent as a small child.

Perspective is twofold, though. While seeing this ugly and brutal side of life, I also was illuminated into the beautiful world of resilience and even forgiveness. I was a doctor taking care of these poor innocent children who suffered terrible abuse at the hands of their parents, caretakers, or whoever was supposed to be the most trusted person in their lives. These kids would bounce back. They would heal, and they would do it all the while wearing a smile. These kids had an amazing attitude always finding a way to look at the bright side of things or look towards the positive in their lives. Not only would they put an optimistic spin on their situations, they also had an amazing ability to forgive. These children did not hold a grudge; they did not sit in their beds at night asking God why these things had happened to them. They did not sit in their rooms at night feeling self pity, or saddening themselves with depressing thoughts. No it was quite the opposite; they would feel better and, for the most part, play or be active. Now not every child was like this, but enough were that it made me take a long hard look at my own life and situation and contemplate what made these kids so incredibly resilient.

One particular day, I was having severe pain due to my RA. It was to the point where it was truly unbearable. I had taken my medication, I had tried to rest, I had done everything in my power to minimize the pain, but nothing was working. Dr. Wiener was working the same shift as I was in the hospital that evening. It was a busy night, like every night in the emergency room, but she noticed something different in my behavior. I had been going through a phase at that time of depressed thoughts, and in all honesty I was feeling pity for myself. My mood was dark, and my attitude was lacking. She pulled me aside that night and asked me if everything was OK. I looked at her, and I was honest. I told her, "No, things are not, all right." I told her that I was sad and depressed and that these feelings were stemming from all different directions. I was scared and confused, and worst of all I was suffering excruciatingly from the pains. As I told her all of these things, it came as a relief almost like a sense of weight being lifted off my chest. I could feel the tears welling in my eyes, but I did not care, I had to vent, and I had to tell someone other than my family how I felt inside.

She grasped me by the arms, and she spoke to me in a parental tone. She was not stern, but she was not sympathetic either. Years of witnessing situations in the emergency room had likely given her a perspective into pain that not many others in this world have or would ever like to experience. She looked straight into my eyes and spoke to me. She said, "Maria, nobody in this world can make you happy other than yourself." I did not know exactly what she was getting at, I did not say I was unhappy, but then she continued, "True happiness comes from within, in order to be truly happy in this world you have to be truly happy on the inside." I started to see where she was going, but still her meaning was not completely clear. She added, "If you feel good on the inside, then you will project this on the outside. Once you do that, then you will have the ability to affect others and make them happy, as well." I now understood. She was basically telling me to take care of myself. She was saying that I needed to get to a point in my life where I did not think about the changes, and where I did not let the pain affect my attitude. I had to grow, I had to evolve, and I had to understand that only I held the power to affect my mood. It was the best piece of advice that I ever received. To this day, I still remember her standing before me uttering those words. I can never forget it, and at the time I felt a duty to take her advice and apply it. After all, she had done so much for me over the course of my education in the hospital that I felt I owed her this small symbol of my gratitude.

That day I vowed to change my perspective. I had seen so much hurt and pain in those children, and yet I never heard them complain. I had seen so much opportunity for anger and bitterness from them, yet they never questioned why they were placed in that situation. Their innocence transcended their age, and Dr. Wiener's experience and advice woke me up to that fact. I could not question anymore why I had this disease, I had it, and I had to deal with it. If these children could take that attitude then I certainly could, as well. It was a time of awakening not only of my disease in its full fury, but also of my will not to let this disease define me. I was in control, and I was going to do all that was in my power to assert that control.

Our lives in New York were hectic. I had completed my residency, and my husband had, too. He had pursued a fellowship in pediatric gastroenterology, and I had decided to pursue two extra years in ambulatory care. By the time we began those programs, both of the boys were in school. Things were definitely hectic, but they were going well. Even though we were busy, we still tried to find a way to have a healthy balance between home and work. Every year when the boys were either on summer or winter break, we would pack the family car and drive down to Florida. It was our tradition, we had friends that we missed, and we knew and loved the state. We always had a plan to move back once we were done with our training, but the further we got into our training the more distant a move seemed. We had lived in Miami, but were reluctant to go back there because of the violence. We never liked the Tampa area and the rest of the state was a mystery to us.

So every year we would pack up, go down for a week and take the kids to Disney, which, like every other kid in the world, they loved. Secretly, my husband and I loved it, too. There were always great memories, and we always looked forward to our next trip to the Orlando area.

Finally, the time came. We were both nearing the end of our training programs. There was no more schooling to be done. We had accomplished our goal, the goal we had set so long ago in Spain of making a new life, a better life for our kids, the same goal, which took us from Europe to South America. Then, once our opportunity had been ripped from our grasp there, our goal brought us from South America to the United States of America, a place that gave us opportunity and provided us with the foundation and tools to achieve our goal. That goal was finally attained. We were both licensed and practicing physicians in the United States of America. It was a great feeling. It was a feeling of success and pride that washed over us. But, that feeling was short lived and followed by a huge brick wall called reality. Great, we'd finished our training, but now what? Good question, and unfortunately we really did not know the full answer to it.

As I said before, we always wanted to move back to Florida, but we did not know exactly where. We took the kids sightseeing in New York, and we went to the Ringling Brothers circus in Madison Square Garden. We took them to the observation deck of the Empire State building. They saw all the major attractions that New York had to offer, and then we made our choice of where we were going to live, based on the influence of a mouse.

That's right ladies and gentleman, we were moving to Orlando. Our reason one may ask? Simple, because that is where Disney World is. We loved going down there every year so much that we decided to make it our new, permanent home. When they heard the news, the kids were bubbling over with excitement. Javier and I were excited also, but there was a level of fear that gripped me, as well. We had spent so long in New York training and meeting colleagues in the hospitals, and we were just going to leave all of the tenure that we had accumulated there. We did not know how the hospitals ran in Central Florida. We did not know what sort of demand there was for our particular type of services in Central Florida either. We did not have a home yet, and we did not have jobs. There would be a whole new round of interviewing, which I feared would bring out some of those insecurities about my appearance that I had been trying to conquer. Nevertheless it was the right decision, it was what we all wanted, and it was what we had to do. So, we packed the family up again, left the home that we had known for six years, and in October 1989 we moved blind for a fresh start in Orlando, Florida.

CHAPTER 6

> The journey of a thousand miles begins with a single step.
> —*LAO TSE*

It is rare in life that people get the opportunity to start things over, a sort of a fresh start. But in our lifetime, we had experienced several of these moments. When one thinks about a fresh start it can be an exhilarating prospect, but it can also be a daunting task, as well. We had made a trek across the Atlantic Ocean to South America for a fresh start in order to begin family life near our childhood homes only to be met with the sobering reality that the home and life that we had wanted to build was not only a passing phase, but also an unattainable dream. We then persevered and made a the difficult choice to leave our families once again, and come to the United States in order to chase what we then considered that unattainable dream. We landed on the shores of Miami Beach and were given every opportunity to become what it was that we had so longed for. With that opportunity came more sacrifice and endless amounts of hard work. We packed up and made our way north for a fresh start, and our chance to take advantage of an opportunity given to us and for which we had worked so hard. Things were beginning to pay off for us, but along the way we hit our stumbling blocks like everyone in life does. While living in New York

I discovered a lot about myself, and we, as a family, discovered our path. We made the necessary sacrifices as husband and wife, as well as parents, to provide the best life for our kids, and we persevered. At the end of six grueling years of countless sleepless nights, insurmountable odds and literal pain that was unimaginable, we made it. We finally made it through our training to accomplish our goals and our dreams.

Now it was time for another fresh start in Florida. I was terrified. I had no idea what to expect in Florida as a recent residency graduate. When we moved I had preconceived notions of the area, and none of them matched up with success for a pediatrician. I saw Central Florida as a haven for snowbirds and retirees. From my experiences, which amounted to what I had seen on television and heard on the radio, I was moving into what amounted to a retirement community. Here we were, me a pediatrician and my husband a pediatric specialist, moving to an area where we believed the average age to be well above 50 years old. To me it was equivalent to buying a Ferrari without an engine, it was a nice gesture and nice to look at, but of absolutely no use. Still, this was the area that we had decided to settle, and we were committed to making things work in Orlando.

We bought a house in a sleepy little suburb of Orlando called Oviedo. The reason we had decided on that area was because of its proimity to the city, but it was still far enough away to be a nice place to raise a family. Along those lines, it was centrally located in an area where we had quick and easy access to all of the hospitals in the area. We had been so used to working at hospitals for the last six or seven years that our initial idea was to move down and find jobs working at an area hospital.

Another benefit of the area was the community itself. At the time Oviedo was a sleepy little town, but it had unprecedented potential. There was a huge influx of families moving into the area, and construction was taking place all over the town. The public schools were top quality, which would equal a massive savings for us in tuition for the boys, and the area seemed fresh and vibrant. It seemed to be the ideal place to start for us and the ideal place to raise our family.

We arrived in a 24-foot moving truck, which my boys had appropriately named the "big mama." As we pulled up into our new driveway and took in the fresh Florida air, things were looking up, and we couldn't wait to start on our new adventure. We had left New York at the beginning of the school year, and our first priority was to get the boys enrolled in school as quick as possible. That process was made easy by all of the friendly people and attentive staff in the school system, which made the transition seamless. After a few weeks of getting things in order, unloading the moving truck and unpacking the boxes, our lives began to take shape in our new home.

My husband had been able to find a job working in the emergency room of a local hospital, while I took the first few months of living in Florida to adjust myself to our new surroundings and get the boys acclimated to their new home.

In those first few months, I took the time to soak in my surroundings. I noticed that for all of the reputation that Orlando had accumulated over the years as a sleepy little retirement, golf town near Disney, the place had much more to offer. The city was filled with parks and activities ranging from nightlife a short drive downtown, to the beach, a 45-minute drive away. Also the demographic of the city was much younger than we expected. I'm not saying that everyone was in their 20s and 30s, living the South Beach-Miami lifestyle, but in our area there were a lot of young couples with young children just starting as we were. This was a source of comfort for us, and it was a sign affirming that we had made the right choice in moving down.

After a few weeks, the kids had grown comfortable in their new home, and my husband had found a good steady job in the hospital. He was expanding his gastroenterology clientele and things seemed generally to be going on the up and up for us. I felt that it was time for me to look into finding a position in a hospital setting, working as a staff pediatrician.

I sent out some resumes and made some phone calls. Almost immediately, I received word from the head of the pediatric department for a local hospital that was located mere minutes away from our home. I thought to myself, "How great is this, we just arrived and already I have a lead on a possible job." Things could not have been looking better for us and for me professionally.

Not only were things working in a professional sense, but they were also going exceedingly well in the sense of my RA. I had come to grips with my disease and its accompanying symptoms. I had accepted my changes, although outwardly I did not care to speak about them, and the pains had again subsided. I had controlled them through medication, rest, and the occasional regimen of anti-inflammatory drugs that my husband and I were advised worked best for my type of arthritis. It was an exciting time, and I was excited to see what type of contribution I could make to my new community.

I worked myself up in excitement for my interview, I reviewed every single possible question that I thought could be asked of me, and I rehearsed the best answer I thought I could give. I felt as though my training in such a fast-paced environment as New York could only bolster my credentials in the eyes of my possible employers, and I arrived at my interview with supreme confidence. Sounds like a familiar story, doesn't it? Unfortunately, as the saying goes, history is bound to repeat itself.

I sat in the office of the chairman of pediatrics, where initially things were very cordial. I offered a little background into my past, my heritage and my training experience in New York. He responded in kind, but after a few brief moments of idle banter he looked at my hands and stared a fixed gaze upon them. It was obvious what he was doing, looking at the changes or the swan-neck formation of my hands, and he stared as though he had lost all interest in everything else. He made no apologies for this, and instead proceeded to blatantly ask me if I had rheumatoid arthritis.

After so long of trying to suppress those intense feelings, which ranged from inferiority to rage with regards to my disease, I though I had made progress by leaps and bounds. I was mortified by the question. First, this was something very personal and very private to me, but apparently he did not see it as so. To me, people have a right to express their personal information to others in the way they see fit, and if I don't volunteer any information, I do not feel as though you have the right to barge into my private affairs and solicit such personal information. It would be like me going up to someone who looked ill in the street, and introducing myself with the follow-up question being what type of illness are you suffering from? To me that type of behavior is not only rude, it is plain old just not right.

I did not know how to react to the question. I really did not know how to respond. To say that I was shocked would be an understatement. I panicked, and I reverted to the old answer that I had used so many times before when faced with this sort of question. I looked the gentleman square in the eyes, and retold the fantastical tale of when I was growing up as a child of how I had been the unfortunate victim of an incident wherein I had broken both of my hands, concurrently, in the same area, with the same outcome from healing. The more I say it now, the more idiotic it sounds in my own head that I actually expected people to believe this obvious and blatant lie. This gentleman leaned back in his chair with a confused look across his face. The look on his face was worth a million words. He did not have to say anything, because I felt as though I could read his mind.

I could literally hear the conversation that he was having with himself at that point in time. His inner monologue almost certainly sounded something to the effect of, "Does this woman take me for a fool?" "Does she really believe that for one second I believe that she broke her hands as a child?" "Does she believe that I am not intelligent enough to know what someone with rheumatoid arthritis looks like, or their symptoms?" If this was not what was going through his head, then it should well have been, because this was what was playing in mine.

At that moment all of my shame, the uncertainty and embarrassment that I had worked so long and hard to try to overcome came rushing back into my life. I believed that I had made unprecedented strides towards self-confidence and comfort, all to be washed away by one simple comment from a person that should have been inconsequential for me. The true depths of this disease and its psychological affect had only begun to unmask themselves. The interview continued, but the damage had been done. I had been put on the offensive, and from then on I was only looking for a way out of the conversation. It had been another of many eye-opening experiences, not only for the social value of the brazen things that people will say on first appearances, but also for the nature of my reaction to what I perceived to be an issue that I had well under control.

I decided that I could not truly be happy working in a hospital setting. The thought of a constant barrage of questions regarding my disease, as well my unwillingness to allow people to glimpse into such a personal side of my life were not a winning recipe for that work environment. I still liked the idea of high-volume work, and an ability to focus on the medical aspect of care instead of the business aspect. So, I began looking for a happy medium. I began looking for a place where I would still be an employee, but I would not have to have interaction with too many colleagues, or people who would ask too many questions.

I came up with several different options. The first was to attempt to get a job at the health department. The health department was a smaller work setting, more intimate with less employee traffic. It seemed like a good idea, due to the capacity in which I would be employed. I would be a staff doctor, whose responsibilities would encompass all medical care for children who came through the clinic doors. But, there were the drawbacks of working for the health department inherent in any bureaucratic endeavor. The pay was less, and the work was monotonous. Being a staff doctor did not entail any of the real challenges that I so enjoyed with my cases at the hospital and, not that the money was the driving force behind my search for a job, but I definitely wanted to be able to make a little bit of money in my profession.

So I continued looking for other options. In my search for a steady job, I began to think about those things that were really important to me, and those things that I wanted to accomplish in my career. I mean, if I had to do something for the rest of my life, I should be happy doing it, right? I began to reassess the goals that I wanted to meet within my profession. I found that inside what I really wanted to do was cultivate relationships. For all of the joy and satisfaction that I got from working in the hospital and helping those kids get better, I felt that there might have been something missing. I came to the realization that part of the joy of being a pediatrician was the opportunity to not only help sick kids get better, but also in seeing healthy kids grow.

I started to shift my search in career opportunities. I realized that I would not get the chance in a hospital setting to see kids grow and mature into healthy adults. I knew that in order for me to be able to become a part of the communal fabric, private practice would be the way to go. I had to become ingrained in the community, or at least become a part of some sort of endeavor that kept in touch with the children of the community. I had gone through interviews at hospitals and emergency clinics. I knew the lay of the land so to speak in the community, and now I had to tailor my search for a private group or practitioner willing to take on another doctor to help them in their mission to provide top quality care for the area's children.

With a renewed sense of purpose, I did just that. I scoured the yellow pages, because back then the Internet was yet to be part of our everyday lives, and I looked into local pediatric groups and private clinics. I found several and scheduled a meeting with the managing partners. During this time, I also made arrangements with several hospitals to be the covering physician for cesarean-section delivery births. I was making money covering these births, and was in no rush to jump into a situation where I was uncomfortable in my surroundings. I met with several groups and private practices, and I just never felt right in any of the settings. For the most part, this feeling was not due to any pressure or discomfort in the lines of questioning that I received. As a matter of fact, after my experience during my interview at the hospital for a staff pediatrician position, I was not questioned with regards to my physical appearance again.

Rather this feeling of not belonging stemmed from something different. I saw how these clinics worked, and how they operated, and no disrespect to them, but they were just not the mold that I wanted to create for the longevity of my career. So I continued looking and looking for the right fit. The deeper I delved though, the farther away my goal seemed to get. I began to feel that I would not be able to ever provide the type of care that I so desired if I had to conform myself and my practice beneath someone else's supervision.

Around this time, I was approached by an older doctor who had been the head of pediatrics in one of the hospitals where I was covering these high-risk deliveries as a pediatrician. We got off on the right foot and hit it off well from the beginning. She told me that she was in the process of opening up a clinic in an area of Orlando closer to the attractions. This was approximately a 45-minute drive from my home, but her offer sparked my interest. She offered me a position working three days a week seeing patients and earning a structured commission on the work that I did at her office. The offer was appealing for several reasons. First, it offered me the freedom to continue looking for a more permanent position while still being able to treat local children and become known in the community. The position allowed for flexibility, as well as a pinch of stability.

I accepted the offer, and I began working at the clinic in November 1989. The experience was great, but the pay structure in the end was a little different from what I had imagined. Regardless, the experience was life changing for me. Being in the office setting in a clinical structure, I felt as though I could let my guard down, and really get to know not only my co-workers but my patients and their parents, as well. I then and there decided that I had to open my own office where I knew I could be in control of things. I would have my own business to build and grow, both personally and with my community.

I set off to speak to my husband about opening my own practice in our hometown of Oviedo. He was very supportive, and we began our search for the perfect location in our community. There was a fairly new shopping center in the center of town that had availability for rental space. We did a little homework and saw that there was a lot of traffic in the area, mainly due to the fact that the only local grocery store was located in there. After a few days of deliberation, we decided that this would be the ideal place to open my practice.

After scouting the location and figuring out exactly how much work needed to be done to build the space up into a presentable doctor's office, we ran some numbers and presented them to the local city bank. I remember being very nervous walking into the bank, because I had never asked for a loan before. I remember wanting them so badly to take me seriously and think of me as a capable professional worthy of their investment. After a few minutes of talking and a few more of listening, the director leaned over the table shook my hand and told me that we had a deal. This bank had just given me the greatest news in the entire world – they were going to give me a shot. This bank was willing to fund my project, and they were allowing me the opportunity to live the American dream. I was overcome with emotion, and I could not hold back my joy. It was truly something to celebrate. With a stroke of their pen, they had changed my life. It seems like a trivial amount in today's perspective, but to me the $4,000 that they were lending me represented more than just a loan. The money represented the culmination of all of our hard work and sacrifice scattered over three continents and 15 years. We had finally been able to put ourselves in a position where we now controlled our own destiny, and, to be honest with you, once the elation wore off it was scary as hell.

I say that only half joking, because now the reality was beginning to settle in. This was the literal basket that I was putting all of my eggs in. If this did not work, I did not know where I would go. I had already decided that I did not want to return to the hospital, I did not want to work for any other physicians, and I did not want to work as a physician for any other organization. My future would depend on how I made it as a solo practitioner in my field. After a few months of build up to the office space, my husband and I hired some help and completed the majority of the renovations on our own. Throughout the building process, I was still commuting back and forth to my other job in the clinic near the attractions in Orlando, and I was also covering the high-risk births at the hospital. After five months of working those jobs, and getting all of the leg work done for my own practice, I was finally ready to branch out on my own and open up shop for myself. In April 1990, Oviedo Pediatrics opened its doors to the public, and I was my own boss for the first time in my life. I was 35 years old, I had two boys, ages eight and 10, a supportive husband, and I finally reached what at that time I had deemed success. I owned my own business in the United States of America.

In the beginning things were rough, really rough. My husband was still working emergency room nights, all the while trying to build his own pediatric gastroenterology practice in downtown Orlando. I was still working three days a week at the clinic and still covering the hospitals, with all of my other time dedicated to building my practice in Oviedo. At times I felt overwhelmed, and I had spots where I would doubt myself, but my will to succeed would not let me keep a negative attitude for long. We chugged along our tough road, and unfortunately, in some instances, our kids bore the brunt of our experiences.

There were nights when my husband would be working the graveyard shift in the emergency room, and I was still covering the hospitals. There were several times during those nights when I would be woken from a deep sleep by the ring of the telephone. It would be the nurses or the staff from the hospital informing me that an expectant mother had some sort of complication with her pregnancy and the doctor had deemed it necessary for the mother and the baby's sake that she undergo a cesarean for delivery. When this happened, I would be notified so that when the delivery occurred I could be in the room to assess the baby, make sure that everything was well and that no further treatment was needed for the child. These were spur-of-the-moment decisions that could happen at all hours of the night, and believe me they did.

Once I received word that the mother was going into surgery, the staff would be waiting for me to come in and assess the child. The only problem was that I had two of my own children at home sleeping in their beds, and I had nobody that I could leave them with. It would be all hours of the night, sometimes 3 a.m. When I say all hours, I mean all hours. So I did the best I could. I would wake the boys up, load them into my car, and take them to the hospital with me. I would put them in the nurses' station while I assessed the child, and then I would collect them again and take them back home to sleep. It was rough for a while, and I'm sure it was rough for them, but we did what we had to do in order to survive.

Another issue began to arise once Oviedo Pediatrics opened. I had to dedicate myself to making this practice a success, and I tried my best. With both of us being spread so thin, and my husband working nights again, we had to figure out a system for who was going to care for the boys. As with many questions, an answer was not that far off. Since we did not have any family or any friends in Orlando, I refused to entrust anyone with caring for my boys. I had a business to run as well, you may say. This is true. So what was I to do about caring for my boys and running my business? Well, logically I put the two aspects of my life together. You see, my boys were my companions, and they were with me always. They were my two little shadows. They were my best friends. I could not bear the thought of putting them in any sort of after-school care, or program that I knew they would not enjoy, so I hired them. Well I did not really hire them, but they became my first employees at my office.

In order to dedicate myself to my practice, I had by this time resigned my position at the other clinic. Although I had been grateful for the opportunity, I knew it was time for me to focus all of my energy on my own business. Along those lines, my boys began to focus all of their energy on helping their mom. I still had a little bit of the startup money leftover from the initial loan, so I began an aggressive advertising campaign. I printed flyers, and my boys would go into the parking lot to put them on the windshields of all of the cars they could see. I printed cards, and my boys accompanied me as I went door to door throughout neighborhoods in the community trying to meet parents, and let them know about their new neighborhood pediatrician. I called their schools, and my boys would help me prepare materials to hand out and that the kids could take them home to their parents to let them know that Oviedo Pediatrics was here. They were great, they were my best friends, and they were a huge source of support for me.

After a while business started to pick up. We would get some walk-ins here and there, and we would get some people who had reviewed our material to come in to see what we were all about. Although business was technically picking up, it was a far cry from having the means to be able to hire someone to help in a receptionist or assistant capacity. So who did I turn to? You guessed, it my boys. They did everything. If the phone rang, they picked it up and took down messages. If I was in an examining room with someone, the boys would mind the front and make sure that anyone who came in received the information that they needed. They did the billing ledgers, and they put the forms necessary for new charts in all of the patients' files. They were efficient, they never complained, and, even more important, they were a source of support that I could not have lived without.

During this time, the pains in my joints had begun to get progressively worse and worse. For some time things had appeared to stabilize, and, after all of the long northern winters, I thought that the mild climate of the south would be a welcome reprieve. For the most part it was, but I think, coupled with the stress of the hectic last few months we had experienced, coupled with the unpredictable weather shift from bone-chilling cold north to humid, hot and muggy south, my body was all out of whack. I remember the pains that I felt, and how bad they were during the days. They had grown to a point where they were almost intolerable. I would try in the mornings to control them with the anti-inflammatory and pain medication as best as I could, but the effects would seem to wear off by midday.

During the afternoon, I would leave the office to pick the boys up from school and bring them back for the remainder of the workday. They would man their positions in the front as assistants answering phones and greeting patients. As they did this, I would go back to one of the two examining rooms and lay down on the table to try to regain strength. Countless times, I would sit on those tables on the verge of tears because the pain was so uncontrollable. I would sob on the inside and all of those old terrible thoughts would creep back into my head. Why me? What did I do to deserve this? The pains had progressed and had morphed into something that was ravaging my very core. My bones would shiver, my joints would swell, and all I could do was watch and try to get a brief rest in those afternoons when my boys would cover for me. They were my angels, my sons. They never complained, and they never turned down the opportunity to help their mom. By this time, they knew that mommy was sick, but they didn't know how sick she really was. I tried to hide the pain from them, but I don't know how good a job I did. All I know is that they always had a smile for me, and they always understood when I needed to leave them to lie down and collect my strength. They also knew how to cover for me when patients arrived and I was not feeling well. I remember my oldest asking the patients to fill out the paperwork, and telling them that the doctor was on the phone in the back so she would be up when she was finished. He would then come to the back and wake me, and let me know that I had enough time to build up my strength because they thought I was busy at the moment.

Oviedo Pediatrics owes as much to my boys' hard work as it does to anyone else. Without those two little guys, I could not have survived that first year. They helped in every sense of the word. They were with me every step of the way building my business from the ground up. I am happy to say that together we made that first year a success, and it allowed our family to continue to build the business in the coming years. As the company grew, I knew that I could not have my pre-teenage boys running the office. Although they were at that young age what I would consider competent office managers already, and I would put their skills up against anyone else's staff at that time, I needed to let them be children.

After settling in Florida and becoming accustomed to the weather and the tropical climate, I was able to control my RA pains once again. I still refused to go to a rheumatologist at this time. You may think that this was stubborn of me, and you would be right. I had my reasons, though. I refused to go to a specialist for many reasons, in fact. One was my previous experience with the first and only rheumatologist that I had consulted in my life with regards to my disease. The only doctor, besides my medical school professor, that I ever consulted about my disease was the one in A Coruna who told me to put a book on the lump on my wrist.

If you recall, this was the man who had nothing but bad news to tell me and even worse predictions for the prognosis in the development of my disease. First, I was going to suffer from debilitating pains.

Second, I was going to be within a few short years so crippled that I would need to use a wheelchair to get around. Third, this gentleman said that more than likely I would need space-age sleep aids, such as a NASA-designed pillow in order to avoid the degradation in my spine that would eventually and unavoidably lead to my paralysis. That was 20 years prior to this point. Ladies and gentleman, allow me to assure you that I was in no way crippled, in a wheelchair, or suffering from pains that prohibited me from getting out of bed in the morning. In fact since that morbid diagnosis that I received as a teenager, I had achieved some impressive accolades if I do say so myself. I even surpassed some of my own expectations. I got married; I graduated from medical school; I moved to the United States of America; I had two children; I completed my residency; and now I was running my own business. So much for his expert opinion!

Another reason that I never sought the further opinion of a different rheumatologist was just as personal. Up to this time, I had been adjusting and becoming comfortable within my own skin. I had undergone some physical changes due to my disease, and I had battled some of the body-image issues that one would expect a woman to experience with those associated changes. I had always had distaste for sympathy from others. It is a personal thing, and I agree that at some points in life it may have even worked to my detriment, but it is as much a part of my personality as my disease itself is.

My experience with specialists was always one of sympathy. They tried to get inside of a patient's situation, and they tried to empathize. Some people need that type of reassurance, some people need that outlet. I do not. I never have, and I never will. This is not in any way aimed to dissuade people from seeking help from specialists or in any way intended as an insult to rheumatologists, or those who suffer from rheumatoid arthritis and seek their expert opinions. In my experience, I just had not had good encounters with the ones that I had visited. I felt pitied, and I felt as though they felt sorry for me, as if I were helpless. This was not the case. I knew enough about my disease, and I knew my body better than anyone else in the world. I felt that with my knowledge of the disease combined with that of my husband and my medical knowledge, we knew enough to control my disease, which, in turn, would allow us to dominate it instead of allowing the disease to dominate us.

So, at this time, this was what I was doing. I had begun taking higher doses of the prednisone again, and I had begun taking higher doses of other anti-inflammatory drugs. They were all within the recommended dosages for what I was prescribed, but this was a little disappointing to me because my ultimate goal was to be completely off medications, or at least down to a bare minimum of dosage. Undeterred, I pressed on. As I was previously saying, my pains were under a little more control, and the business had grown rather rapidly in the first year. Insurance companies were sending me more and more patients, as I was quickly building relationships with parents and the businesses of the surrounding community. Now I faced an even greater challenge. How was I going to tell the boys that they no longer were needed as my helpers in the office? How was I going to tell them that the business had grown, and that now I did not need them any longer to answer phones, and do all of the other important chores that they did so well? Most of all, how was I going to react to not having them around all the time? I had grown so used to them being with me that I had forgotten what it was like not to have them there.

I had grown used to seeing their little faces around every turn, and, as I said earlier, they literally were my best friends. I could trust them with everything, and I genuinely enjoyed their company all day. But, as the saying goes, all good things must come to an end. It really was not that dramatic of a scenario, though, because they needed to focus on school, and it just made sense for them to be allowed to spend more time at home and playing outside like other children their age. So, I made arrangements with a neighbor to take care of them after school for a few hours until I came home. Now I had another problem, where on earth was I going to find someone to help me run my office? I needed someone with experience, someone I could trust, and someone with integrity and honesty. One problem was we did not know anyone looking for a job, let alone anyone who had experience in a doctor's office.

Interestingly enough, and as life always seems to do, things worked themselves out. One day, while running around like a chicken with my head cut off as I tried to see patients, answer the phone, schedule appointments, take payments and do everything else necessary around the office, I received a visitor. Not just any visitor, but someone who would later become one of the most special people to ever enter my life.

It was one of those typical Florida days, a beautiful morning, followed by a fast approaching and violent afternoon storm. In the midst of the storm, I heard the bell of the front door open. It was around lunchtime, and I was not expecting anyone to be in at this time. I made my way to the front of the office to greet whoever had just come in. As I made my way around the front doorway that led into the waiting area, I saw an older woman standing there soaking wet. I said, "Hello," and she roughly asked, "Is Dr. Miller here?" Needless to say, it was not a perfect match at first glance. I immediately became defensive and informed her that I was Dr. Miller. I was thinking, "Who is this woman, she doesn't have any kids with her, and she obviously doesn't know me?" She continued in her rough manner, "Are you looking for any help here?" I was really put off by her manner, but I responded, "Yes, actually I am." She then informed me that she was looking for work, and if I had a job, then she would take it. I had not even offered this woman any job, and I had no idea as to what her experience was. But, for some reason and against all common sense, I decided to offer this woman a job in my office. And thank God I did.

Her name was Laura Johnson, and she became the best friend that I ever had in this life. She was about 10 years older than me, and she had lived the life of a military wife. She had resided everywhere from New Orleans, to Italy and had the stories to prove it. She stood no nonsense, but she was also the most caring person that I knew. She was fiercely loyal, and she would go on to become one of my most trusted confidantes in the world.

Whatever she lacked in medical experience, Laura made up for with tenacity and persistence. No favor was too great for her and no task too small. She did everything I asked, and she did it without complaint. If the office was busy and the boys needed to be picked up, Laura would go to get them. If I was feeling ill and my pains were too much for me, she knew, and she would cook dinner for my family. She quickly became more than an employee, and she took a vested interest in my boys and in my family. That woman had a heart of gold, and on a daily basis she would put it on display.

Oviedo Pediatrics continued to grow, and it grew at a rapid rate. Things were going well for our family, as well. We had both found success in our respective practices. We were establishing ourselves in the community, and we were growing as physicians. My practice was growing at an astonishing rate, so fast indeed that I was outgrowing my office. We were seeing more and more children on a daily basis, and they literally could not fit in the waiting room. So, soon enough, we were faced with the prospect of upgrading. We purchased a plot of land and built an office near to our home. This building would become the permanent home of Oviedo Pediatrics. It is still there to this day and is where I go to work every day. As an integral part of the success of the business, Laura came along, too. She was promoted to the title of office manager, a title she didn't really care about, and we continued to grow together. Our relationship grew, and she continued to be an integral part of our family.

After a year in the new office and a relatively prosperous time in our lives, my best friend Laura was rocked by life-shattering news. After a routine doctor's appointment, and for the most part a clean bill of health for the majority of her life, Laura would now be forced to face the most difficult challenge of her life. During a routine colonoscopy, the doctor found a mass in her rectum. Initially it went untreated, but after time and discomfort upon her return the doctors decided to biopsy the mass. When the results came back, they came back with the worst possible news that one could ever expect to hear. Laura was suffering from colon cancer.

It was fairly advanced, and she had to undergo radical and invasive surgery to remove the mass. Laura underwent the surgery. She had the mass removed, but the surgery took a harsh toll on her body. She had to be fitted with a colostomy bag, and she still had to undergo further radiation and chemotherapy treatment in order to try to combat the effects of the cancer. Even being sick, Laura came to work every day that she could. She was dedicated not only to my practice, but she was loyal to me as her friend. She wanted to help me, and her selfless gestures never ceased. Eventually, things got to a point in her treatment where she could not continue to work on a daily basis due to the effects of the treatment.

She persevered still, and fought the cancer as best she could. Whenever she felt a little better she would come into work and do as much as she could to help. By this time in my eyes, she had earned the right to come and go from work as she pleased. She was a fighter in every sense of the word. She never let the cancer get her down, and she was always in good spirits and never questioned why she had to go through this process. It was truly an awe-inspiring sight to see the positive attitude and the strength that this woman displayed. After her treatment and therapy, we received good news that her persistence had paid off.

She returned to work, and things went back to normal around Oviedo Pediatrics for some time. Business-wise things were going exceedingly well. The new office was already paying dividends, my husband's practice had taken off, and the kids were growing up quickly as children tend to do. We had been able to build a new house in the same area as our previous house. The kids were already in high school, and Javier Jr., as a matter of fact, was in his senior year. He was almost ready to graduate and move on to college. Things had literally flown by so fast. We were in shock to see how quickly the kids had matured. It was a wonderful sight, but it was also a strange feeling to see your kids gain so much independence before your very own eyes.

Late in the summer of 1995, we again received some bad news at Oviedo Pediatrics. Laura, whose cancer had been in remission for quite some time, received word at one of her regular check ups that the cancer had returned. It was back with a vengeance. The cancer, that had ravaged her insides, was back again and had spread like wildfire. It was devastating to her and her family, but it was almost as equally devastating for my family and me. The doctors gave her a very bleak prognosis. They were now measuring her lifespan in months, not years. They informed her of some dramatic new techniques that might have been able to extend her life and buy her a few more weeks, but Laura refused the treatments.

She resigned herself to the knowledge that this was the path that God had chosen for her, and she embraced it. Besides, even if her life could have been extended, the doctors made no guarantees as to what the quality of that life would be undergoing these radical treatments. So, instead she chose to press on and embrace the beauty of life for the remainder of her days. For a few weeks, she was still able to come to work in good spirits. After that, it became increasingly difficult for her to be mobile. That spring, when Javier Jr. graduated from high school, she made it a point to see one of her little guys walk across the stage. She made it to our house afterwards to celebrate with us like the family member that she was.

We remained as close as could be, and this entire process was difficult for everyone. It was incredibly difficult for me. This woman had been a lifeline for me. She was an oak tree in the office for me to lean on when things were rough, and she had been a sounding board for me to unload on when I needed to vent. She was fiercely protective of my family and me, and, I believe, she truly loved us. People like Laura Johnson come along once in a lifetime. It is our job to either recognize them and embrace them, or allow these rare gems to slip through our fingertips. I'm glad to say I embraced my opportunity to know someone like her, and I cherished every moment of it.

When it became too difficult for Laura to leave her home, I would go over after work two or three times per week. We had our little tradition of sharing a glass of wine on her back porch, and watching the Florida storms roll through. She loved the smell of the rain, and the rhythm of the storm. The intricate dance of the lightning and the thunder was like a well-timed orchestra for her. It was one of my favorite things to do, going over and spending those afternoons with her.

Laura passed away in 1997 after a long and hard-fought battle with cancer. It was an amazing thing watching her fight. I witnessed her struggle with her disease from beginning to end, and I could not but help to draw comparison with her struggles and my own. Although my disease was vastly different from hers, I watched in awe as she lived her life to the fullest. As I said before, she never complained. She always had a positive outlook and never once blamed anyone or questioned anything with regards to why she had to suffer. It was actually directly the opposite, she embraced her fate, and she did the best she could with the hand she was dealt. I saw the raw emotion that exuded from her when she was given her chance of survival, and those sorts of real feelings are an amazing force to see.

She never gave up, and she always persisted right to the very end. I can honestly say that nobody ever knew the pain that she felt, because she never complained. She was close to God, and she knew that eventually it didn't matter what happened here, because she was destined for a bigger and better place. I truly believe that she arrived in that place, and all of her pain and all of her challenges here in this life are being rewarded in the next.

There is a small, separate manager's office in my practice. It is where the filing and the billing are done. As a small token of my appreciation for Laura, after her death I placed a sign on the door to that office that is still there to this day. It is a simple gesture to show my gratitude for her, our friendship and all of the hard work that she also put into building my practice. The sign reads "Laura's office." Along with that little sign a picture of her still hangs there, as well. It may seem like a small gesture, and in reality there is no measure for what she really meant to me, but I feel as though it is my own ongoing tribute to such a special person.

Around this time a lot of other things were changing, as well. Javier Jr. graduated from high school and was now on his way to college. Danny was entering his third year of high school, and was becoming more and more independent. Like any mother, I remember the day my oldest son left home. It was nighttime, and we drove him to school at the University of Florida. The entire family loaded into the car with him, and we packed all of his things in the trunk of the family SUV. We made the hour-and-a-half drive north, and unloaded his things into his dorm room and said our goodbyes. I became overcome with emotion. I could barely look at him as we were leaving because, although he was already 18 years old, the only thing I could see was that small little baby that I carried in my arms to Miami those short few years ago.

Yes, things were changing all right, and no matter how hard you try you can't stop time from going by. Two short years later, which seemed to go in the blink of an eye, my husband and I were making that very same trip with Danny. He had graduated from high school and had also been accepted at the University of Florida, following in his older brother's footsteps. Again, we loaded up the same SUV, with Danny's things this time, and made that same trip an hour-and-a-half north. We arrived in Gainesville and made our way to his dormitory. Again, I was struck by a feeling of emotion for which I could not have prepared.

As we unloaded his things, his entire life flashed before my eyes. I remembered the excitement that my husband and I felt when we learned of the pregnancy as new emigrants in this great country. I remember the suspense we felt when we arrived at the hospital not knowing the gender of the baby, and I remember the elation we felt when we found out that it was a healthy baby boy. All of the good times and the hard times that we experienced as a family sped by my eyes as we unloaded that truck in the very same parking lot where we had stood just two short years ago. This time, I was leaving my baby; I was leaving my little boy. I could not face the fact that both of my boys had grown up.

I mean, we both saw in our boys what we had experienced ourselves and what seemed like yesterday. They were embarking on their lives, they were ready to move on and find themselves. They may have been ready, but I was not. It's tough on parents when their kids grow up. For so long I had been secure in the fact that I could protect my kids from anything. If there was ever any trouble, I would be there to defend them. If there was any advice that they needed, I could provide it. If there was any confusion or anything puzzling them, I could be there to provide the explanation they needed at a moment's notice. That was all gone now that they were gone. They had accomplished so much, and it was time for them to move on with the next step of their lives. They were in a place that I remembered being in myself, as a young student going back to Spain. Those feelings resonated with me, but I still felt like the protective mother. That night in Gainesville in 1999 was one of the hardest nights of my life. It was only 90 minutes north of our home, but to me it could well have been across the country. I was about to embark on a new phase in my life at the same time that my boys were embarking on a new phase in theirs. My husband and I were now empty nesters.

I could barely bring myself to say goodbye to Danny in the parking lot. Javier Jr. had driven over from his apartment to greet his brother and welcome him to college, but I really did not feel like sticking around. I hope that it did not come off as me being dismissive, or in any way that I did not care, because it was the exact opposite. I was in a rush to leave because I could barely handle the moment. People deal with grief, stress, and other emotional factors differently. In this situation, I chose to run from it. I did not want to prolong the inevitable that we would be returning home without either of our kids that night.

Upon our return, things were different at the house. It was difficult to adjust for me. I remember hearing the noise of Danny in his room with the television on when I would get home, or him outside playing basketball, but now there was silence. I remember the familiar sights of a house filled with his friends, or his car parked outside, but now those were not there anymore. I remember going into both of the boys' rooms and looking around just to get a sense of how it was when they were small and always there. I dipped into a slight depression, but I never really cared to tell anyone about it.

I had had dealt with pain my entire adult life, but now I was experiencing a different kind of pain. It was a pain derived not from my disease, or from any psychological effect from my changes. No, this was a pain derived from maternal emotion. I missed my boys, I missed my little musketeers. We had spent so much time together as they were growing up that there was a huge void now. What made this feeling worse was that my husband and my kids were the only real family that I knew. They were certainly the only family that I had been close to for a very long time. Now that family dynamic had changed, and it was just my husband and me at home.

The depression that I felt began to settle in, and I avoided conversation about it, or I would try to hide my feelings for the better part of a year. I had picked up habits in order to try to keep busy, and did the best I could to keep myself occupied. I thrust myself into work, and the best part was when the boys came home to visit. We would spend weekends at home as a family, and share dinners and conversation about school. They would spend time with their friends, and, gradually, those old familiar sounds would again fill the home. Even though the sounds were temporary, they still filled me with joy and helped carry me through till the next time my boys came home.

I know I am making it sound as if my kids going to college, which is an exciting and proud time for any parent, was the worst thing to happen to me. I apologize for the theatrics, because that is not my intent at all. In reality, it was an extremely proud moment for me, but it was a very difficult time, as well. You have to remember, we came to this country with nothing in our pockets and nobody to lean on for any type of support. My husband and I were tremendously proud of our kids. Nonetheless, when you are so close to your family, especially your kids, any dramatic change in the family dynamic is bound to have both positive and negative effects on a person. How that person chooses to deal with those effects marks how they will grow, learn and adapt to the new dynamic.

The way I reacted, as I previously stated, was to immerse myself in my work. After some time, namely a little after the first year, I began to accept our family's new direction. I actually sort of began to embrace it. Thankfully, work had been steady and, after so many years of growth, Oviedo Pediatrics was continuing to expand. I had witnessed a lot of my patients over the previous years grow from babies to children and now begin to move into their teenage years. It was a great source of joy to be surrounded by these families and their children on a daily basis.

I had begun to sense a feeling that I previously had only felt at home. At work, in front of all of my patients and my work environment I was comfortable. Not only was I comfortable, but I was also confident in myself. I began to notice that I carried my head a little higher in my office, and I was a no-nonsense doctor when it came to these children's care. The change must have been gradual, but noticing that change came in what seemed an instant. I no longer felt the shame associated with my disease. I did not feel any stigma, and I did not feel any eyes gravitating to the physical signs of my disease. I was open and honest with the parents of my patients. Long ago were the days where

I would try to hide the root of my appearance behind lies of childhood misfortune. Now I would tell those who inquired about my disease and all that it entailed.

I met parents who were suffering from diseases similar to mine, and I also met families who had suffered through medical tragedies that were much more sudden and traumatic than my own rheumatoid arthritis. Unfortunately, in pediatrics there is that off chance where a child is ill, and there is nothing that can be done to save that life. I have had this experience only a few times, and you can never get used to it. As a physician, it is a helpless feeling not to be able to care for this person, who you feel you are supposed to bring back to health. As a mother, it is a feeling that you hope to never feel. No matter what you say to that parent, there are no words that can bring comfort. The only thing you can do is offer your support and let the healing process begin to take hold. This is easier said than done, and luckily I have not had too much experience in this aspect of medicine. I say not too much, but in reality any such experience with an innocent child is too much.

In this vein, I began to engage the people around me more freely and speak about my personal health issues with an open mind. People listened, and it helped me become a better doctor. My patients and their families began to realize that nobody is immune to health issues, and everyone has their own battles to fight. I remember a little girl coming to my office who was diagnosed at a very early age with rheumatoid arthritis. Her physical changes had already begun to take form, and her pains were tremendous. She had been to specialists, and she had been on medication, but she had difficulty dealing with the mental aspect of our disease. It was difficult for her to comprehend the limitations associated with it, and she was having a hard time accepting her physical capabilities. I knew her pain, and I knew her struggles. The outside is what people can see, but the fight that wages inside of one's mind when dealing with this disease is invisible to all. The day I met her was a life-changing experience for me. This little girl touched my heart.

Her family had noticed my physical changes in my hands and my elbows. They were so polite that they tiptoed around asking me if I, too, suffered from RA. In the past, this question would have been met with immediate denial, followed by an attempt to cover my hands and arms. Then, it would be on to some ridiculous attempt at explaining exactly why my appearance was what it was. This time, I engaged them in conversation. I informed them that, yes, I was living with RA, and that I had been doing so for practically my entire life.

The family was full of questions, and I was glad to answer them. As someone who had navigated life with this disease, I felt the least I could do was be honest with this young lady and somewhat prepare her for the trials and triumphs she could expect. Leaving that visit, I felt that the little girl maybe could feel a little better about herself, knowing that there were others out there just like her. There were others who knew her pain, and others who had dealt with her emotions themselves. I felt good about myself with the thought that maybe I was able to make her feel good about herself. I told her to never be ashamed and never let anyone tell her she could not do anything. Things might take a little more effort, but there was nothing in the world that anyone else could do that she couldn't.

She became a faithful patient of mine, really more because of her parents doing than her own, and some months and years later I would come to find that our initial meeting had made more of an impact than I had originally thought. It turned out that this young lady, as she has now grown up to be, has decided to pursue a medical career of her own. As I write, she has graduated from high school, is enrolled in college, and has been doing exceedingly well, I am pleased to report. It seems that, prior to our initial meeting, this young lady had been struggling with our disease, but in me she saw an example of what can be achieved. Her parents informed me that she saw me as sort of a role model, or some personification of normalcy for herself. Someone who struggles with rheumatoid arthritis has a duty to redefine what normal means to him or her. There are limitations to one's abilities, but those limitations can be minimized and marginalized. It seemed that by being open and honest with this young girl showed her that anything is possible, as long as you do not allow this disease to define you. In a way, I feel that I may have been able to bring her definition of normal and her prospect for a bright future closer to her grasp.

Stories like this began to take shape on a routine basis in my office, and I began to feel more and more comfortable within those office walls. The safety and the comfort that I had only experienced at home, was transferred to my office everyday with me. I felt good there, and I felt as though I could be free from the shame and embarrassment of my disease. I owe my patients and their parents a debt of gratitude for that. Not only did they trust me enough to care for their children, but they were a source of therapy for me, as well. I guess it could be said that, as I was helping them and their children get better, they, too, were helping me get better. They provided a haven for me, a sanctuary where gradually my insecurities about my appearance in public gradually disappeared. I began to be able to deal with the mental aspect of my disease in a much more productive way, at least in the closed walls of my office. This was leaps and bounds greater than where I was just a few short years before as a mortified resident in New York who would stop at nothing to avoid any and all conversation dealing with the shame I felt as a byproduct of my disease.

Things are never as simple as they may seem, and when one problem begins to be resolved, there is always another to confront. As I said, I had never returned to a specialist to diagnose me, or treat my RA. I had always relied on over-the-counter medications, or medications that were prescribed, or samples recommended by colleagues with expertise in the area. I had tried to avoid any of the heavy-duty medications, such as prednisone, due to the extreme reaction to the medicine that I had experienced in Spain, and the side effects that could possibly result from use.

Things were changing now. I had gotten a little bit older, and the pains were becoming gradually more intense over the years. They had begun to intensify when the boys still lived at home. With the distraction of having the kids around and building the business, it had not been too great a change. Even then, I would just take an extra Advil, or consult a colleague with regards to my current prescriptions. There were times that the pain was unbearable. By unbearable, I mean torturous and mind numbingly unbearable. During these times, I would do the only thing that I knew to do. When modern medicine did not work, and no amount of care would do, I prayed. As I will discuss later, I have always had a special relationship with God, and I have leaned on him through the good and rough times in my life. He has always been beside me, and I am a faithful believer in the power of prayer and the guidance he provides.

Even when you turn to prayer and ask for signs, you cannot turn a blind eye to the obvious. My RA was acting up. I was experiencing greater pains. Those pains were lasting a significant amount of time longer, it took a much larger dosage of medicine to control the pains and get them to subside. In order to relieve some of the agony, I found myself having to turn once again to prednisone, a drug I never wanted to use again. My husband saw the pain I was experiencing, and we did everything we could in order to try to alleviate it. Things were not working. Around this time, we had decided to take a family cruise to Alaska. It was a great way for our family to come together and spend some quality time. But the pains were so bad that it jeopardized my ability to go on the cruise. I did not know if I would be up to the travel and the exposure. Since some of my medications were dosed only to be taken once or twice a month, I began making deals with myself. I would allow myself to suffer longer for one week, so that I could extend the relief provided by the medicine to a later week so that I could experience greater relief in times of my choosing. This was no way to live. I was basically forcing myself through extended misery only to be provided with temporary relief. But that is exactly what I did to salvage our family vacation. It was a great trip but, upon our return, things were different. I felt defeated. Those old feelings of shame, guilt and plain pain began to creep their way back inside of me. My mood deepened, and I began a very dark period of my life.

It was around my 47th birthday that I took what I considered a turn for the worse. It was 2002, and Javier Jr. had already graduated from college. He had been accepted to medical school and was currently home on vacation. Danny was a junior in college, and much had changed during that time. The boys were no longer boys and no longer awkward young adults. They were men, but we all still shared a strong family bond. The boys knew that the previous few years had been tough for me, first with their departure, and also with the growing pain that I was experiencing due to the disease. There was nothing really that they could do except to utter words of encouragement, and they always offered their support. My husband knew my pain because he had seen me suffer through it for over 25 years. No matter what we tried, nothing worked. We both tried to figure out a suitable regimen of both exercise and medication to control the pain, but nothing worked. We raised doses, nothing. We tried new drugs, still nothing. It was an exercise in futility, and anything and everything we tried was basically useless. Nothing worked, nothing eased the pain.

My disease was back, it was not only back, but it was back with a vengeance. I literally tried everything that I could, and I began to fear that I was doing more harm to my body than good. I struggled through the year as best as I could, and then rock bottom hit for us. In November of that year, my husband's father was scheduled to have heart surgery in Colombia. He was older, but the surgery was deemed to be one that he had a great chance of survival. The details of the surgery I really don't know, but what I do know is that he did not make it through the operation. My husband was devastated. Our family had not had to deal with a major tragedy like this yet, and we were not prepared. Of course, we had moved away from them over 20 years before, and we were not as close as we would have liked to have been, but he was still his father, and it was devastating.

My husband and I sat on the back porch that night smoking cigarettes and reminiscing. He made arrangements to fly to South America and attend the funeral. He returned a few days later, and we tried to get back on with our lives as best we could. It was a difficult time for both of us.

Then, two weeks after the news of my husband's father's passing, I received a phone call at my office. One of the assistants found me in an examining room, and informed me that someone was on the phone from Venezuela and that they needed to speak to me immediately. The only family I had in Venezuela was my parents, my sister, and her children, so I immediately went to the phone to make sure everything was OK.

At first, I feared something had happened to my parents on the road because there had been incidences before. My parents maintained their shoe sale business through the years, but had eliminated the factory element. What they did now was more of the transport duty of the operation. A few years prior to this phone call, they had been making their way home in their truck from one of their travels when they were suddenly stopped and carjacked by a band of thieves. These disgraceful cowards held my parents at gunpoint and robbed them of their life savings. After robbing them, they bound and tied them to a tree with their hands behind their backs and left them on the side of the deserted road. My parents were pleading for their lives, and they were spared. My mother's medication, on the other hand, was taken, and with the stress of the situation my father worried for her. After the attackers left, he freed himself from the tree and walked barefoot to the nearest station in order to call for help, so that my poor mother, who was still abandoned on the side of the road, could be checked and treated. These despicable swine said something to my parents that evening, which they retold to me and which will forever be stuck in my mind. They kept repeating to each other not to shoot or hurt my mother or father because their boss had told them not to. These men were less than scum, but whoever hired them obviously knew my parents, knew their routine and knew they would be carrying cash with them. Whoever hired these people was the lowest form of trash on this planet.

Fearing a repeat incident, and knowing the very real possibility of its occurrence since the original thugs had not been apprehended, I made my way to the phone and answered as quickly as I could. What I was about to hear I could not have prepared for in a million years. It was the type of news that nobody is ever prepared for, and my family had to hear it twice in two weeks.

When I reached the phone, I greeted the person on the other end. It was my sister. It would be very difficult to describe our relationship, since we are so far apart in age, and I never really spent too much time with her growing up. It would be difficult to say that we are close. It would not be difficult to say that we are close enough that when I heard the tremble in her voice that day I knew that something horrible had occurred. She could barely hold herself together long enough to form sentences, and I could barely make out the words interrupted by sobs and elongated pauses to catch her breath. Finally, she was able to get out the gut-wrenching news.

Earlier in the day, my parents had left their home to begin a weekend of deliveries for their clients in the mountains. By all accounts, it was a beautiful day, blue skies, no clouds in sight and generally an inauspicious afternoon. After packing the merchandise in the back of the truck, my parents had loaded themselves into the caravan and began their long journey to their vendors. It was a long ride, but a ride that they had managed countless times before throughout the years. It began like any other weekend trip for sales. Traffic was normal, the weather was great, and there was nothing really remarkable about the day at all. They had made good time loading and leaving the home and were expecting to arrive at their destination in good time. With their early departure, it appeared that they were well on schedule, and no rush or hurry was needed on their part.

Here, the story became convoluted. Apparently, my parents were making their way over a bridge where there had been an accident or some form of road construction. As they approached, there was a vehicle on their side of the road. Noting the vehicle on his side of the road, my father grew concerned. Well before the vehicle was upon them, my father took evasive action in order to avoid a collision. It appears that, as he was making a turn or trying to go around some further oncoming traffic, he was blinded by something momentarily. In that split second and in his blinded confusion, my father overcorrected the wheel of the caravan and drove the truck right off the side of the highway. Apparently, the area was rather flat off the concourse of the highway except for a large tree, which unluckily the caravan hit. The head-on collision between the vehicle and the tree was so great that it forced the truck to topple over on its side.

The scene was catastrophic. All of the merchandise was spilled across the roadway – one shoe here, a shoe over the bridge, and others scattered in traffic. Glass shards littered the ground, and pieces of automobile were strewn across the asphalt. Boxes reached as far as the eye could see, and sitting in the passenger cab were my elderly parents. Miraculously, my father was uninjured. He undid his safety belt and tried to come to my mother's aid. He tried to wake her up and was successful. It appeared that she, too, was uninjured in the fracas. By this time, a bystander had alerted the authorities of the accident. The sirens could be heard well off in the distance, and it appeared that my parents, by some divine luck, had avoided any serious injury resulting from the accident.

By the time the authorities arrived, my parents had already exited the vehicle and begun assessing the damage. My father had begun trying to collect the merchandise that was still intact, as well as recover what he could from the merchandise that was scattered about. The medical team had assessed my mom at the scene. She had been complaining of pain in her side and her abdominal area since the initial impact. Deeming it serious enough to warrant transport to the hospital, the first responders loaded her up into the ambulance to have her checked by a doctor in the emergency room. My father dutifully followed behind the first responders to accompany my mom in the ambulance to the hospital, when she reached out and stopped him.

My parents had been workers their entire lives. As I said before, my father left Spain for Venezuela in order to find work and provide a better life. My parents were not afforded the luxuries of education and opportunities that I had been afforded because of their hard work. They had a routine, and their routine always involved hard work. Throughout life, they had been dealt some very difficult hands, but somehow they always persevered and found the light at the end of the tunnel. They were not wealthy people by any stretch of the imagination, but they were also loath to accept handouts or assistance from anyone. They were proud people. This accident was seen as only another stumbling block on their path through life. The merchandise spilled in the roadway was not only seen by them as their savings and their responsibility, it was also the collective savings, responsibility and, ultimately, the source of income for all of the vendors relying on its delivery.

Therefore, as my father tried to follow my mother, being lifted into the ambulance on a stretcher, she reached up and grabbed my father's arm. She told him not to leave the merchandise behind. They had worked too hard to see anything happen to their life's work again, as it did the night they were robbed. She went on to tell him not to leave the truck by itself either, because if someone came and stole it, they would be left with nothing. Hearing this story, and retelling it to you breaks my heart. Here these people, my poor little parents, who had provided me with every opportunity in life, were concerned with such an insignificant matter as shoes on the road. To them it represented so much more, though. So my father stayed. He waited for the police to arrive as the paramedics rushed my mom to the hospital.

On the way to the hospital, complications arose. The pain that my mom was experiencing was due to internal bleeding. The bleeding could not be stopped, and the impact was so traumatic that the internal injuries were spewing blood at an uncontrollable rate. As my father waited for the police to arrive to file a report and tow the truck to a safe location, my mother was being transported to the hospital in the back of an ambulance, and she was bleeding to death.

My mother never made it to the hospital. She died in the back of that ambulance, surrounded by strangers. It is one of the saddest memories that I have in my life, if not the saddest. My father had no idea as to what had happened in the back of the ambulance that day. When he arrived at the hospital, he was expecting to see his wife of so many years, battered, bruised but responsive, just like she was at the scene of the accident. Instead, when he arrived, he was welcomed with the news that would effectively shatter his life. His companion through life was gone, just like that in the blink of an eye. It destroyed him.

The news hit me like a sack full of bricks. I was floored. I literally dropped the phone and began to weep. It had been a long time since I had seen my parents, but I had maintained a great relationship with them. Through the years we kept in touch, and, even if we could not physically be near each other, we always stayed in contact. In the recent years since the boys had been gone, and we were had been enjoying relative success with our practices, my husband and I were discussing the idea of attempting to spend more time with our parents and families overseas. Within the last two weeks all of that changed forever. That opportunity was now gone, and taken in the most violent of ways.

My husband and I made arrangements immediately to fly to Venezuela so that we could help my father with any necessary funeral plans. He was a different man from the one I remembered. As the driver, he held a lot of guilt inside of him. He also held a lot of guilt for the entire sequence of events throughout the day. As I reminded him, and I continually had to remind myself throughout the entire process, God has a plan for all of us, and this was just part of God's plan. My mother was gone, she was buried in a small cemetery near my parents' house in their small hometown, and in the span of two weeks my husband and I were taught a valuable lesson in regards to the fragile nature of life. In some senses, it seems like we walked through tragedy together. He had always been by my side with my disease, but he never felt my pain. Two weeks earlier, when he lost his father, I was the one who did not know what pain he was going through. In one of those cruel ironies of life, we now had to deal with the same pain at the same time. We helped each other through as best we could, but we had our own way of dealing with such a devastating loss.

The boys never really knew their grandparents, so they did not register the immense loss that we felt. They knew that we were hurting as anyone would be when a parent dies, but they did not have that connection that most children have with a grandparent.

Upon our return from Venezuela, life went on again. We rhythmically fell back into our existence at home, but inside things were not right for me. I took the death of my mother very hard. The entire sequence of events surrounding her passing had a really devastating effect on me. Coupled with the increased and intense pain stemming from the disease I had been feeling for quite some time now, I sank into a deeper and darker state. I began to lose my appetite. I then began to feel lethargic in the morning. The thing that kept me going through all the years, my office, began to take a back seat in life. Things were so bad that I was no longer even able to hide my pain at work. Throughout the day, the parents of my patients would notice me looking down and looking glum. They would ask me if I was OK, and I would always say yes. Towards the end of the day, it was more difficult. The pain and the stress were beginning to show on my face. It was impossible for these people, who I was supposed to be caring for, not to notice the suffering that I was experiencing from my disease. I hated that I could not hide it from them, since this was not something that should have concerned them. My pain was a distraction for me, and it affected my mind. I was losing interest in my career, I was suffering, and I was in utter and crippling pain.

One day, I was seated alone at the kitchen table. My son Javier, who was home from school for the weekend, came around the corner and saw me staring and lost in thought. I must admit, it was not a state that I wanted either of my kids to see me in. I was scared. For a few days prior, I had been truly taking a long hard look at my life. I was analyzing myself. I remembered when I was a young girl feeling the pains and making deals with God to live to a certain age. I looked back at all the things that we had accomplished and how far we had come. I began thinking to myself that maybe these feelings were not only pains from my RA, but something else might be going on.

Never in my entire life had I felt such ravaging pain for such a prolonged period of time. I could not bear to think what could have possibly been going on inside my body that could make me hurt so badly. I thought the worst. My emotions got the better of me, and my son sat with me at the table. He implored me to go to a rheumatologist and seek some medical help. It was time to allow someone else, other than my husband and me, to decide on what was the best course of action to treat my disease. I gave in. I agreed to go see a specialist and get a full physical. I agreed to this not only for my son's sake, but also for peace of mind and for my sake.

I made an appointment with a local rheumatologist. Quickly, I remembered why I did not like going to doctors to speak about my disease. My husband came with me to my appointment, as he always did. Instantly, I was transported back 30 years to another time and place. I felt like I was back in Spain. I felt the same way I did when I went to my first and last appointment with a specialist. Even though, this man knew I was a practicing physician, he treated me as though I was a victim. He questioned me as to why I had not come to him sooner, and chastised me so I would know that he held the power to heal me. Never mind the fact that I was also a doctor, he made me feel inferior as a person. He was utterly disrespectful and uninterested in what would make me feel comfortable. He tried to assert his will and force me into a regimen of medications that included injectable drugs. I refused, telling him that I did not do well with needles, and I knew there was a certain type of drug that came in pill form, which I was interested in using first.

My husband and I grew angry as he tried to continue to persuade me to follow his recommendations. I refused, and we both voiced our opinions in an assertive tone. Finally, he relented and agreed to prescribe me methotrexate in a small dose. I had heard about the drug as a medicine used in high doses with cancer patients, but it was also used in small doses as a medical treatment to control the effects of RA. As I left the office that day, I vowed never to return to that man again. The visit opened an old wound from Spain that I thought had long healed, but when you deal with people who only want to treat illnesses and not people, those old wounds find a way of splitting open very quickly.

I began my regimen of methotrexate, and I continued using my anti-inflammatory medication in small doses, as well. I felt as though I needed the guidance of someone with more knowledge of these medications as I began to take them. I decided to go to another rheumatologist, a woman this time. I made an appointment, which my husband and I both attended. When we arrived we were smack in the middle of the same scenario that we always seemed to find ourselves in. I was taken to a room where this woman wanted to take copious amounts of X-rays of my hands, why I don't know. It was plain to see my physical attributes, I was not there to inquire about surgery, and I did not want to change anything physically about myself. I wanted to deal with my pain, and, needless to say, she was not too interested in what I wanted, or had to say.

I never returned to either of those doctors. Please let me reiterate here that I am not speaking ill or generally about rheumatologists. As in any profession, I am certain that there are some really outstanding physicians in this field. For me, though, I just did not feel comfortable with the ones I had the opportunity to see. I decided to go another route. I had been taking the medicine for a few weeks, and I was beginning to notice a change. I felt a little better, the pains were dulling, and I was regaining the strength and function that I had previously had.

I did my own research into the medication and became aware of its possible side effects. Armed with that knowledge, I began to undergo regular checkups and blood work, to make sure that the medication was not in any way negatively affecting me. I also began speaking with patients and specifically the parents and grandparents of the patients that I knew suffered from RA. They were always a great inspiration for me, and also, I had come to find, they possessed a wealth of knowledge from which I could readily draw. In conversation with some of these families, I had repeatedly come across the same recommendation. Many of the families told me about this fruit drink that they swore by, it was all natural and made from the acai berry. The drink had tons of vitamins and minerals and, to all intents and purposes, was extremely healthy. That was not the reason I was interested, though. The reason I was so interested was because these people kept swearing that it helped reduce and relieve their associated arthritic pain.

I thought about it, and I came to the conclusion that I would try it. I mean, these people had put their blind faith into me to take care of their kids for years. The least I could do was put a little bit of trust in their advice. Also, it was an all-natural drink, so what the hell could go wrong? I received my first shipment. Around this time, Danny began running long-distance races. He would suffer from those typical aches and pains in his joints that all runners feel. In doing research of my own, I came across another product that was all natural, and high in glucosamine and chondroitin, which are good for joint recovery and injury prevention. I started buying it initially for both of us. I mean, I think someone with RA could use a little joint recovery and injury prevention, as well as a distance runner. Frankly, at this point I was willing to try anything to get rid of these pains.

I had commenced this regimen fully expecting it not to work. It was sort of a last-ditch effort and a way of conceding that I had finally begun to truly experience the full force of the disease. But, a funny thing happened along the way. My pains began to gradually subside, and my spirits began to lift. I had recently celebrated my 48th birthday, and, knock on wood, it seemed like I might yet see better days. As a gift that year, my husband had bought something extremely special for me, and it was something that would come to be irreplaceable.

I thought that he had forgotten my birthday, but he gave me flowers and a card. We celebrated with dinner and did all of the usual accompaniments for celebration. For weeks, he kept saying that he had something to give me, but he could not give it to me yet. I thought, "Sure, he probably forgot and has not figured out what to give me." Boy was I wrong. It seems the reason he could not give me my gift was because my gift had just been born, and I could not get it for eight weeks. That's right – my husband bought me a puppy for my birthday, a little golden retriever puppy that we named Maverick. He was the cutest little ball of fur that anyone could ever imagine. When my husband brought him home, he was so tiny and so helpless that it really was the sweetest little sight I had ever seen. His little spirit for adventure took him all around the house, but he would trip up over his overgrown paws and immediately run to my side when he was intimidated by something. It was almost as if I was his safety blanket, and he did not want to stray too far away from it.

We had had another dog in the family which we had purchased in New York and who had passed away a few years earlier. His name was Eric, and he was a golden retriever, collie mix. He was a great dog, but he was a very independent animal. Eric lived 16 long years, but unfortunately passed away from cancer. It was a very painful sight to see him suffer, and I vowed never to buy another dog for that reason. I can't bear to witness an animal suffering, and suffer he did.

Maverick was different from Eric in the sense that he was not independent. He always wanted to be near people, and he loved any form of attention he could get. There is something to be said about the companionship of animals and their therapeutic nature. Animals are used in all settings to assist people in all sorts of recovery, be it as therapy dogs for sick children in hospitals, to service dogs for the handicapped in the community. Now trust me, I am not accusing Maverick in any way of being any sort of service dog. You can barely get him to stand still for one minute, let alone convince him to bring you anything. He has trouble with the retrieving part of golden retriever, but everyday we come home there is one constant. That is that there will be a happy face and a wagging tail waiting excitedly to greet us at our door.

This was the beauty of my gift. It was something to care for other than myself. I had not had that feeling on a daily basis at home since the kids left, and now I had it back. I knew that there was something else relying on me to care for it, and if I did not take care of him, feed him and protect him, he could not survive. Maverick was the greatest birthday gift that I ever received.

It had been a few months, and I had adhered to my new medical regimen. I took my doses of the new drugs, as well as combined them with the natural remedies from the juices that I had begun taking on my own. The results were amazing, I felt like a brand-new person. Initially, I thought that this was some form of introductory phase of the medication, and my body had not been used to it. I believed that this may have led my body to overreact and feel an initial sense of positive change. The longer I took my medications and my natural remedies, the better I felt. Time continued to pass, and I continued to feel better and better. My health exams came back positive. My health was better than ever, and my pains had diminished.

Soon enough, not only had my pains diminished, but I began to regain strength. I had begun to be able to do things that I had not been able to do in years. I began to take Maverick for long walks in the neighborhood, without feeling any ill effects later in the evening. I was able to take him outside and play fetch with him in the yard, even though he still had a little trouble with the retrieving part of the game, God bless him. Little things in life that used to be impossible for me were now commonplace and easily completed tasks. For example, remember when I told you about the time in New York when I refused to sit in the park with my kids out of fear that I might not be able to get back up. This utterly embarrassing inability to perform such a menial and simple task had plagued me my entire life. Now, I found myself rolling around in the grass in the backyard with my dog and playing with him in the sun as if nothing could bother me. I could get up and down with ease, and not suffer any ill side effects from the motion.

I had been feeling so good that I got a little daring. There were risks of increased side effects associated with the regimen of medication that I was taking. Luckily, I had not, to date, experienced any of those side effects, but that was not to say that I was not exposed to them and could possibly suffer some form of setback with age. I had put my full faith in my natural remedies, but I was not crazy you must understand. So, what I did was, I decreased the dosage of my medications gradually and increased my intake of my juices. Gradually, I was able to eliminate the prednisone from my regimen, and I was able to get the dosages of my two remaining medications to the lowest that they had been in my entire life. I felt great, also. At no point have I ever felt any ill effects from the elimination or the gradual decrease of these medications, and, to date, I have been pain free for almost seven years.

Don't get me wrong, there are good days and bad days still, but they are just that, good and bad days. Long have been the days when I dread waking up, because of the pain. Long are the days of avoiding certain activities because of the possible painful repercussions that I may face.

This is not an infomercial for any of the products that I adhere to, but to tell my story without at least mentioning them would be to tell an incomplete version. I am in no way saying that natural remedies are some form of lifesaver, or fountain of youth, but what I am saying is that these things worked for me. Without them, I do not think I would be in the position that I am today. For the first time in 30 years, I am no longer conscious of the daily rigors that my disease brings. I am in a peaceful place. After weathering a storm that lasted for almost three decades, I have arrived in a harbor which offers clarity and peace of mind. I am in a place where pain is an afterthought, and self-imposed limitations are a thing of the past.

During this seven-year journey to health and rejuvenation, a lot of things have happened in our lives. A lot of things have happened in the world, as well. My oldest son, Javier, is now a doctor himself. He is married to a wonderful young woman, whom he met while in college. In fact, a little piece of information that I neglected to mention earlier is that when my husband brought Maverick home, the next day my son and his wife bought Maverick's little brother. They were the last two puppies in the litter, and they are the best friends that I could ever ask for, besides my husband of course.

Danny is now a lawyer and is also married. He married a young lady whom he has known since high school. She is a pediatric nurse in the Orlando area. The boys have migrated home in their older age. The entire family lives in the Central Florida area. We are still very close, and we talk on almost a daily basis. I do not have any grandchildren just yet, but I have my hands full with my two puppies. Soon enough, I am sure that our family will grow, but I am in no rush.

I can honestly look in the mirror today, see the person that I have become and truly say that I am proud. When I see my family, and I look back on our journey, I can say that we have become something. My husband and I began a journey so many years ago that admittedly had a much different ending than we had first envisioned. Along that journey, there have been so many obstacles that were unforeseen. It is amazing to look back on our lives and think about the seemingly insurmountable challenges we actually had to face. Those challenges are what defined us as people, as well as parents. Success was always our goal, but the definition of success changed along the way. The idea of success to us was a fluid concept that adjusted with our current situations.

Early in our lives, we defined success as doing well in school; it then shifted to career goals upon graduation. Soon thereafter, it was defined in family goals. The point I am trying to make here is that, just like anyone else, we had to adjust our way of thinking, and the way we measured our lives changed, as well. I finally arrived at a definition that I think is universal. It is a definition that has served me well for the last few years, and it is simple enough that I can apply it to all situations. I believe that success should be measured in quality of life. It goes back to what Dr. Wiener told me all those years ago. I wanted to take her advice immediately after hearing it, but sometimes in life it takes a while for your actions to catch up with your intentions. She was right; as long as you are happy inside then everything in your life will follow suit. Success is measured in happiness, and as long as you are a happy and productive person, then in my eyes you are a successful person. Your station in life does not matter one bit, from garbage man to neurosurgeon, from child to elderly person, we are all equals. The only thing that matters is how we feel about ourselves, and how we project those feelings. To be a truly successful person you have first to be happy on the inside.

I am living proof that persistence pays off. I do not feel as though I am anything special. I do not think I am the smartest person, or the strongest person, but what I want to express to everyone is that those things do not matter. We came to this country with a suitcase filled with clothes and a dream, and we achieved that dream. Of course, there were bumps and bruises along the way, but those only served to strengthen our resolve. Everything we have achieved we have done with one eye on success and another on failure. We defined our successes along the way, and denied ourselves the decision to contemplate defeat for even an instant. When I was down and in pain because of my disease, I pressed on. My family picked me up, my husband and my boys carried me through. When one of them had a difficult time, the rest of us banded together, and we helped that person out. I think that has defined our ultimate success. A team is more than just the sum of its parts, and, as such, our family is a championship caliber team. The great thing about families is that they all have the ability to be that sort of championship caliber team.

As I have said, I have been relatively pain free for the last seven years, and, God willing, I will continue to feel this way. I have arrived at a place of peace with my disease, as well. Long ago, I stopped allowing my disease to define me, but along the way I had many mental and physical battles with my disease. I have not conquered my disease, but I have learned to live with it. Along that road, I have arrived at a place of tranquility with it. I still have my times where I feel those insecurities associated with the physical aspects of my affliction, but when those thoughts creep into my mind, I remind myself that I am above that. The people that matter in my life do not see me in that way, they only see me as Maria the person, not the victim, and that is all I ever wanted.

CHAPTER 7

Faith is being sure of what you hope
for and certain of what you do not see.
—HEBREW 11:1

R eligion, unfortunately, is such a controversial topic these days. When we look back upon it, religion has always been one of those topics that has inspired divisive rhetoric and inflamed passions. Since the beginning of time, history has been full of wars and bloody battles waged in the name of religion and God. Persecution has always been the unfortunate step-mate of faith. The ancient Romans persecuted Christian and fed them to the lions in gladiatorial times. More recently, bloody massacres of the Muslim peoples were initiated in the name of the church throughout the Holy Wars. Over the centuries, the Jewish people have been persecuted and exiled in the vilest of ways, for example, the holocaust, all in the name of religion.

It is not only these religions that have suffered. The Dalai Lama has been exiled from his homeland for years simply because of his religious belief. With faith there is pain, but without pain we would be unable to feel the joy and the comfort that faith also brings.

Faith rings true for all religions; whether Jew, Christian, Muslim, or Buddhist, no matter your affiliation, faith is a deeply spiritual and personal thing for all people. I myself grew up a Catholic and have been one for my entire life. I have remained a practicing Catholic, but I have been exposed to and have seen the beauty in all faiths. I would like to share my experience and my faith with all of you with the understanding that, because I am a practicing Catholic, I see the beauty in all religions. I do not feel that any one is better than any other. With that being said, the common thread that runs through all of our religions is the strong bond that we hold dear to our hearts. It is that closeness that lifts us through hard times, that one thing that we know we can always turn to in life, which will never let us down. Faith is not a crutch, it is a gift. That same gift humbles us in good times, and it allows perspective to flood our lives again.

My relationship with God began when I was a very young child. I came from a family that was not overly religious. In my small village, survival was the overwhelming theme of my youth. God played a role, but church was not a staple of the people's daily lives. I mean, we would celebrate the holy days and everyone had a deep sense of faith during that time, but attending service was not all too common.

I remember being a little girl and asking my grandfather to take me to church. He would walk me to town, and he would take me to the physical location of the church. While I went inside and listened to the priest giving mass, which was still in Latin at the time, my grandfather would sit at his cafe drinking his seltzer water or coffee and watch the television to see if there were any soccer matches currently playing. Church was also a unifying theme for me. When my grandfather was unable to take me to town, I would ask my grandmother if she would take me. She rarely left the house and almost never went to the town, but in those rare instances when I would ask her to accompany me, she would. I enjoyed that time with my grandmother. Our journeys to and from church would allow us to share moments that we would otherwise have been unable to enjoy.

During my early years, I began to associate God and faith with good things and good times. Christmas, for example, was and still is a favorite time for all kids, and I was no different. For some reason, I continued to be drawn to church spiritually, and I enjoyed all of my experiences there. I remember having conversations with God as a little child, and those conversations were, as you would expect, innocent in nature. I would say my prayers and ask for little things, nothing major, and I always felt good leaving church knowing that I stopped by to say hello.

When the time came for me to join my parents in Venezuela, my whole world had turned upside down. The only home I had known was being taken away from me, and realistically the only parents that I ever knew, my grandparents, were being ripped out of my grasp. As a young child, I was confused; more than that I was angry. I really did not have any friends to speak of, so I turned to the only person that I knew that I could always talk to; I turned to God. I spent countless nights asking him why I had to leave, why I had to move, and, more importantly, why all of the sudden I could not see my dear grandparents any more. I talked to him nightly, and the more I spoke the more he listened. That is the great thing about faith, even though you cannot have an active conversation with someone, you know in your heart that this person is listening to your every word. You can feel the presence, and it can be extremely comforting. This is how it was for me, and, as time passed and as I adjusted to my new life, I felt at peace with my surroundings, and my God had brought me to a place of understanding and tranquility.

It was an early lesson that spoke volumes in my trust and my faith. After asking questions, I was provided not with an explanation, but with comfort and an open ear.

As I grew older, my faith grew along with me. Things in my life began to take a more complex turn, and along with those complexities my relationship with God became more complex in nature. I continued to go to church religiously, pardon the pun, in Venezuela. Although my parents were not particularly religious people, they were supportive of me and my beliefs. I was enrolled in a Catholic school, and I excelled in my religious, as well as my secular, studies.

The time came a few years later when I would begin to rely on faith in a different way. Fear is one of the most powerful emotions that a person can experience. For many, fear of the unknown is the ultimate example of fear. We fear what we don't know, in large part, because we do not understand that which we do not know. When we are ignorant about something it causes an instinctive response within us, it triggers basic primordial responses rooted deep within us – responses, such as the flight or fight response and, worse, an instinctive desire for protection. We try to provide ourselves with this protection even if we are unable to find it. We hide from within and withdraw from the outside world.

When I began feeling the initial symptoms in Venezuela brought on by my disease, these responses began to take hold. I knew that I was different from other kids. I knew that there was something that prevented me from doing the things that all of the other children who surrounded me could do. I did not know what it was, and I was scared. I was scared, but I did not want to express my fear. I did not know how to express my fear, so I hid it. I internalized my emotions, I buried them deep within. The only person I could turn to was God. He was the only person I thought could understand. So I spoke to him often. I began making deals with him. I began negotiations with him for my life. I was so scared that my time would be cut short on this planet, not so much for my own sake, but for the sake of my parents and my family. I was terrified, so I prayed.

Prayer has always been a haven for me, a sanctum where I could always turn in times of need. I prayed for a deal, I prayed for God to give me some time. He responded, and I was granted the time. Once I got to the age that I had prayed for, I returned to him in prayer and asked for an extension. He kindly obliged.

When I left my family in Venezuela once again to return to Spain, it was a tremendously difficult time in my life. I was saddened because I did not want to leave them. So, I turned to my faith, and quickly I was comforted with the realization that I was supported by not only my family, but also my God.

When I was diagnosed with rheumatoid arthritis in Spain, and I was faced with my own mortality as a result of the prognosis from the doctor in A Coruna, I was shaken, but I remained confident that my faith would carry me through. As a matter of fact, it would be years before my faith would again be shaken or tested. I had promised that I would never allow anything to get in the way of my relationship with God, but there came a time in my life when I began doubting my conviction seriously. Throughout my life, I had questioned whether or not my disease was a result of some form of punishment from above for some transgression unanswered for; those feelings were always quickly dispelled through faith, prayer and confidence.

Throughout all of our years in Spain, throughout our entire ordeal in South America as our life seemed to be in a shambles, even through our early years in America, I knew that God had a plan for us, and I never wavered in my faith. There were tough times, and there were times of great elation, but, throughout all of those periods, we knew that through faith all things were possible.

When we returned to Florida after living in New York, I entered a dark phase of my life. As I described, I went through a period of intense pain and uncertainty as to how my disease was progressing. I remember turning to my rock again, to my strength and savior. I prayed for an answer, for some help, for some relief to the pain that I was constantly enduring. I tried everything, and there was no relief forthcoming. I could not bear the pain, and I could not bear the suffering, not just physically but also mentally. I began to feel that possibly the well had run dry, and I had relied on Him too many times. I began doubting myself, and, in turn, I began to feel that I might have doubted my faith.

I remember being in Church with my children one weekday evening. It was a special service in which the priest had called those suffering from a chronic disease to come forward for a special blessing. I went forward, and I got in the line. I was in so much pain that it was even difficult for me to get out of the pew, but I did. I struggled forward, and approached the priest. He asked me what my affliction was, and I responded that I suffered from rheumatoid arthritis. He reached over and blessed me, and said a prayer over me. I returned to the pew and released a torrent of emotion that I had not felt in a long time. I felt lost, I felt shame, and I felt rage – rage at myself for questioning the one thing that had carried me through my life all these years, shame that I would question my savior in any of his decisions or his actions, and lost because I still was living with this excruciating pain.

As he always has in my life, God provided answers. I hear people speaking of wanting signs and expecting miracles from the voices of the beyond. I have always found my answers in the simple things, such as a coincidence or a suggestion from a friendly stranger. These are the ways that in life I have been able to use as the vehicles of my faith. Ever since I stopped asking why and began listening to life for my answers, I have never doubted my faith again.

My mother's passing was also a difficult time for me. Although difficult, my resolve was not shaken. It was actually the exact opposite; my faith was strengthened in this ordeal. I spoke with God, and I asked him to care for her in Heaven. I asked him to be with her and guide her to be reunited with all of those who had joined him before her. Also, I began to see a new side of my father as a result of this incident. Tragedy can do one of two things. It can shake your faith and lead you to question motives and events, or it can strengthen your resolve and put your faith in something that can relieve some of the pain from the grieving process. With me, it did the latter. Fortunately, for my father it appeared to do the same. Although he still, to this day, visits my mother's gravesite with weekly regularity, it appears that he has made peace with her passing as have I.

Prayer has been pivotal in my life, and my relationship with God has always been a dynamic and evolving one. I have always spoken to him and have gone to him and asked for advice and counsel throughout my life. There came a time when I thought that, maybe, he had grown tired of my requests and my constant questioning. I thought that, maybe as I said earlier, all of my favors had run out. I hope it does not seem like I have only turned to God in times of need because, although when faced with difficult times I have always sought his advice, I have always praised him and thanked him in good times. I have always had continual and constant faith, and I hope that our relationship is a symbiotic one.

I have never really known how to express my gratitude and the extent of my appreciation for the wisdom I have gained from his counsel. I have come to the conclusion that the only way is to live a good life. I have tried to live a good life, and I have tried to be a good person. I am not a perfect person by any stretch of the imagination, but I do not think that is what He is interested in. I have raised a wonderful family, my husband and I have lived lives that I think we can be proud of, and I try to use the wisdom He has given me in my everyday life by helping sick children.

I believe that the only thing that God has ever asked of me, and has ever asked of anyone in return for his ear and his advice, is for us to listen. We have to listen, even when we do not want to hear what it is that He has to tell us. His advice is not always the easy path, or the path of least resistance, but it is the most rewarding. I wholeheartedly believe that I have lived the most satisfying and gratifying life that I could have lived. It has been filled with struggles, as well as triumphs. My life has covered the highest mountains, as well as the lowest valleys, and the great thing about it is that it is just beginning in my eyes. I hope to have many great years to come.

I have been reborn with age, and, just recently, I feel as though I have been able to shed the cocoon of shame that followed me for so long. I am in a good place, and I am finally able to say that I am proud of the person that I have become. If I am able to help or inspire anyone, even one person with my story, then I will be satisfied that this project was a success. There are so many people in the world suffering and internalizing their pain, that if I inspire just one person to speak freely and see that they, too, can achieve anything as long as they are willing to put forth a little effort and believe in themselves, then I will have succeeded.

I am living proof that once someone puts their mind to something, all they need is perseverance and faith. The rest will take care of itself. I want to express that I am not anyone special. I am only a person who arrived in this wonderful land with a dream, determination and drive. With that we have carved out our own little success story. If there is anyone out there who does not believe that they can achieve, or anyone who is in a dark place, I hope that my story can ignite a spark of inspiration in them. In the times that we are currently facing, I know that it is difficult to see the light at the end of the tunnel, and that is exactly what inspired me to write my story. As women, as well as those in the Hispanic community, we are all too often confronted with and shown examples of our failures. I want to show that even in these dire times we can achieve, we can have success, and we can persevere.

It is a difficult time in our world and faith has carried me through, faith in my God and faith in my family. They have been my rock and my reason for everything. My life has been a constant series of lessons being learned. Sometimes those lessons have been difficult, but they were always well worth the knowledge. I hope that my story can provide some inspiration to all who read it, and, if anyone has any questions or advice, you all know where to find me – my second home, and the place where I go every day to help others in the same ways that God has helped me.

AFTERWORD

This note comes from the author's son and co-writer.

A sk anyone who has ever sat down and written a book, and they will tell you it is no easy task. To actually sit down at the computer and hammer out the words is a tough and long process. You have to be mentally in the right spot, as well as dedicate the necessary time to express yourself in a coherent way. This was my first attempt at such a feat, and I hope that I did this topic justice and presented it in not only a cohesive way, but also an entertaining one.

Tackling this task was something that I did with a little hesitation. As children, you always think to look at your parents as these indestructible beings who have amazing super powers. They are our protectors. If we ever need anything, they are there to provide. Whatever it may be, in the form of food, shelter, or emotional support, our ingrained reaction is always to turn to our parents for guidance and protection. When we are small children, these larger-than-life people shape our lives, and, as we grow older, our relationship changes with our parents, but our perspective of them usually remains the same.

I have always been in awe of my parents and the accomplishments that they have been able to achieve. I have always known generally their story of success in the United States. Mind you, I was born in 1981, and I don't really have any clear memories of life until we had already left Miami and had been well settled in New York for quite some time. Even so, my memories from that time are few and far between. I knew that my parents were doctors, and I knew that they worked a lot. Other than that, I thought our life was normal. I had friends at school, and I just figured their lives and their parents were the same as mine. I loved my parents, and I revered them, but I did not think that there was anything about them or us that made us stand out, or made us any different from anyone else.

As we grew older, my brother and I learned more and more of our parents' struggles. We realized that we were not the typical family. We realized that our friends led much different home lives from ours, and we had questions to which we never really knew the answers. As kids tend to be, we were a little self-centered and wondered how come we didn't know our grandparents, how come we were not surrounded by family, and where exactly was Spain, Venezuela, and Colombia? Were these places so far away that people did not want to visit? Then we discovered these wonderful things that people called maps, and quickly those questions were answered. Still some questions remained, such as if they were all over there, how did we get here?

With age and maturity, we learned more and more about our parents, little tidbits of information about where they went to school, how they met, and how they eventually got to the States. These answers were typically vague, short and to the point, not out of any desire to avoid the subject on behalf of our parents, but rather a necessity for brevity as there are so many aspects of their ordeal that, well for lack of a better term, could fill an entire book.

So I knew where my parents were from, and I knew why they were here – simple enough, right? Well, underlying those simple answers there were some tough and complex questions that I did not realize I needed to have answered until I was approached with the idea of helping my mother write this book. I knew everything about my parents with regard to them being my parents, but did I know them as people. After all, from what I already knew, they had lived quite an exciting life prior to me even being born. They had lived on three continents, had visited several countries and were already accomplished physicians. Some would think that they had already racked up enough experiences to fill a lifetime. But after that, with one child already, they moved to the U.S. where I was born. It all sounds pretty crazy when put into perspective.

Then there was the other side of the story, the not-so-glamorous side that although only physically affected one of them, had been something that they had both been dealing with for a long time.

Growing up, I had noticed that my mom was a little bit different from other moms. The first thing you notice when you meet my parents is that they speak with accents. They both speak impeccable English, and in my perspective are two of the most brilliant people I have ever met, but I'm biased. Regardless of this fact, they do both have heavy Latin accents. That's one of the things that in initial conversation you pick up on with my parents. The other thing that is immediately noticeable as a first impression is my mom's physical appearance. To me my mother is one of the two most strikingly beautiful women that I have ever seen, the other is my wife, but on the surface there has always been something different about her.

As a child, I always wondered why my mom's hands did not look like everyone else's hands; I always wondered why her feet did not look like everyone else's feet and what those things on her elbows were. I wondered, but it never dawned on me that these things that I saw every day were signs of an incredibly painful and debilitating disease. As a child, I asked her what they were, and I knew she had arthritis, but telling a child that is like explaining nuclear physics to a two-year-old. They will look at you, but your voice is just passing noise through their heads. I had no idea what rheumatoid arthritis was, and I had no idea that my mom was in constant pain. Quite the opposite as a matter of fact, I had never really seen my mom exhibit any type of outward pain growing up, I just knew that she had arthritis, and that was why her hands looked the way they did.

As I got older, I began to understand that my mom's arthritis was a little limiting, and her condition made it a little more difficult for her to do certain things. Still I did not fully grasp the idea of the disease, or its full effect on those who suffered from it.

You can understand my original hesitation in becoming part of this project. I knew my parents as just that, and I was not sure if I wanted to know any more. There was a world and a life that they had apart from the world I knew, and I just was not certain that I wanted to know more about that world.

However, after further discussions and a little cajoling from my mom, I decided to go along this journey through the past with her. I am glad that I did. The insight I received from my mom into the world that she had occupied opened my own eyes, and allowed me to meet the person that she really is. We started by doing little interviews around my parents' house, and she filled me in on aspects of her childhood and her past that I had no idea about. She walked me through my own ancestry and brought to life areas of Spain in a different time and a different place that I would have never known. She introduced me to family members that I had never heard of and, unfortunately, would never get to physically meet. She spoke of people who were so influential, not only in her life but also in the lives of both my parents. Hearing stories of a mischievous little girl in rural Spain, allowed me to relate with stories of myself growing up as a small child.

Although we know that everyone is a child at one point in their lives, for me it has always been difficult to picture my parents as children. I believe kids get those images from grandparents, who tell tales to grandchildren of how their parents behaved as children and various incidents that happened. Sadly, my brother and I did not have that luxury. This was also a point when exactly who my grandparents were came to life for me. It was amazing and a little disheartening to hear the story of struggle and simplicity that they lived. I knew that my mother had lived with her grandparents as a small child, but I had no idea of the reasoning behind it. Hearing the tale being retold by my mother in her own words was both sad and inspiring to me. It showed both the necessity to adapt to the human condition, as well as the tenacity of the human will to persevere.

As we delved deeper into her story, I began to understand my mom a little bit better. As I said before, until this point she was not so much a person, she was just my mom. Now she was developing an entirely different identity in my perspective. After continuing to collect information for the project and learning more and more about the specifics of my parents' lives as young adults, I began to relate better to them, as I am now in that stage of my life. Learning the difficulties that they endured as young adults, and the fact that they endured these struggles thousands of miles away from any sort of support from home, made their story that much more inspiring. It put a lot of things into perspective for me, and it made me realize how lucky my brother and I truly are. No matter what our struggles, or what hurdles are laid before us, we have always known that we have the full support of our parents within arms' reach. It is humbling for me to realize what they went through, and there is no way for me to compare situations. The only thing I can express is gratitude for their never-ending love and support.

As we continued on our journey through my mother's life, I began to discover more things about her. I think it is the goal of all parents to shield their kids from harm and always try to put a positive spin on life. It's funny, as a kid I don't remember my parents complaining about anything. I never remember hearing my mom ever tell me about her disease, and I surely never heard her complain of any pain. It was actually quite the reverse; growing up I never looked at her as any different from anyone else. I mean, I knew that there were certain things that looked different, but she never acted as if there was anything wrong, she never complained, at least not outwardly, and she certainly never asked for special consideration from anyone. So, as we sat recalling her life and she described the onset of her disease and its painful progression, I was left stunned to find out the extent of the pain that she had endured.

I had heard the term rheumatoid arthritis my entire life. I knew that my mom had it, and I knew that it was something she lived with and dealt with. But I did not know exactly what rheumatoid arthritis was and how it affected the person who lives with it. I certainly never considered it a disease, because growing up disease had such a negative connotation to the word. I associated it with sick people, who were always ill, lethargic and always in pain. My mom was the farthest thing from that. She was always vibrant, young and full of energy, but that's what parents do – they shield their children from pain, even if it is their own excruciating pain.

As my mom opened up to me and described her ordeal with the disease, a new light began to shine upon her. The in-depth tales of her and my father learning about the disease as a young couple, and them attempting to grasp the full measure of all that it would entail, was truly awakening. Then, her further tales of their journeys for remedies and treatments as young students in order to control the disease was inspiring. It was inspiring because it was a revelation for me to see and hear that as young people they, too, struggled in their relationship and faced hardships, but they persevered. It showed me a side of my father and mother that, up till that point, I did not know. Their persistence was motivating, and the lengths to which they went were unfathomable for me to comprehend.

Hearing their tales of cross-border trips and weekend visits to doctors to understand what was happening also provided a deeper insight into the bond they share. My parents are different now from the people they were then. In my estimation, they are successful, they are older, and they are more refined, but hearing stories of their rugged youth and angst shed a different light on them.

Furthermore, accounts of their successes in Europe, such as graduation and having their first child, enabled me to hear in my mother's voice something that I do not believe she even noticed. The sense of joy and pride she exhibited when speaking of their small family and their small home in Spain was comforting and inspiring. I am in a similar situation now with my wife, and knowing that roughly 30 years ago my parents were in the same predicament as we are gives me hope for the future. I mean, these people did everything with virtually no help and support, and as a result I see where they are now and the success they have achieved. With that knowledge it would be presumptuous and almost downright arrogant of me to feel that I have it worse in any way.

The first time I ever truly heard the story of how our family arrived in the United States was when I interviewed my mother with regards to that event. I sat down with her that day, and I was prepared for an average emigrant story. Maybe something about the American dream, or something about job opportunities, you know something inspiring, but nothing that would be too outlandish. What I got in return was a tale that I could not wrap my mind around. I had had no idea what my parents had to go through in order to arrive in this country. I guess I have always taken it for granted; after all it is the only home that I have ever known. The way we got here, though, makes me appreciate their efforts more and more. To think that I should have been born in Venezuela or Colombia or somewhere other than the United States to me is about as foreign a concept as there could possibly be, but, as retold to me, this was the original plan.

As you have read, my parents endured a lot in their search for a home and happened to come upon the United States in the same way a lot of people come to these shores. The search for their home and their tale enraged me. In all honesty, it lit a fire in my belly that was so strong and so potent that it literally made me sick.

I am proud of my heritage, and I am proud of where my family comes from, but to hear how my parents were treated in what amounted to their homeland saddened me no end. The way they were dismissed and pushed aside truly ripped my heart, but still they continued trying. When I heard the story of the guard at the border putting a gun to my mother's head, I was livid. I could literally feel the pain and fear in her eyes. It is easy to imagine how she felt, and it affects her even to this day. I could also feel the rage, and helplessness that I am sure my father felt. That sort of rage does not come along very often, but when it does it is the sort that could drive a sane man crazy. I was angry, I was sad, and I now had a new-found respect for my parents and their struggle.

Their resourcefulness was epic, and their drive to succeed was obvious, so when they told of their idea to come to the welcoming shores of the United States I was not surprised, but their description of how they arrived did shock me a little bit. It takes courage to arrive in a strange land with no money, no family, no knowledge of the language or culture, and no way of knowing if and how you are going to make a living. Compound that with the responsibility of a child already born and another soon to come, and that seems to be a recipe for disaster. Instead, it was fuel for their success. To take what life had given them and make proverbial lemonade out of those lemons is a truly uplifting tale. That was only half of their journey, and the rest of their tale provides examples of their resolve throughout.

The thing that I take away from this experience the most, though, is the pain that my mother has lived with for over 35 years. As I previously said, I always noticed the physical differences that she had, but to me it was not a big deal. Growing up, it was never really mentioned, and if anyone ever asked we would just say she had arthritis. It's amazing now looking back on it how that explanation just seemed to work. I do not ever recall getting any follow up questions from friends, or any need for any further explanation of what arthritis was. So to me, at least, her disease was a non-issue.

As she sat there retelling me her stories of countless morning and days filled with physical pain, the layers of her life began to unfold before my eyes. My mother was no longer just my mom, the lady who raised me and one half of my adult role models. She took on a whole other persona. She was complex, strong and full of life. She had had experiences that I had never known about, some that I could all too readily associate with and others that I could not even imagine myself encountering. Her physical pain was immense, and expressing it seemed difficult, but, even more arduous for her was allowing herself to open up and describe the emotional pain that the disease had thrust upon her. It appeared as though expressing the actual depth and degree of what she had endured in an accurate form was close to impossible. In the beginning, words seemed to fail her, but as we went on she was able to describe how she had finally been able to shed the cocoon of pain and shame that she had been experiencing for so long.

There was this cathartic transformation that began to take shape and occur before my eyes. It opened me to a world that I had never known. I had no idea about the extent of my mother's pain. I had no idea of the mornings that she suffered and the days that she anguished. As I continued to hear her story, certain emotions began to run through my body. I finally arrived at a place of awe. I was, and still am to this day, inspired by the strength that my parents, and particularly my mother, possess. She is the strongest woman I know. The struggles that she has endured and the fights that she has taken on are mind boggling.

Her story was humanizing. It broke down life into its simplest form. When stripped of all of the dressing, it is a story of survival. At a time in her life when people's perspective is measured in nightly plans, instead of future goals, she had to face a diagnosis of an unimaginable consequence. When fear would be the only proper way to describe what she was feeling, she made a decision to attack the issue head on. Instead of running away from a problem, she tackled it and sought help to control her pain. When my parents were looking to start their lives, they were thrust into a situation where they were shunned from a land in which they thought they would grow old. When faced with unimaginable obstacles in starting anew in a foreign land, they stared any and all fears in the face and proved the depth of their character.

As I said before, I knew the general outline of my parents' history, but the detail with which it was retold to me was awe inspiring. To know that they were not given anything, nor did they expect any handouts from anyone made me swell with pride. To know that they rolled their sleeves up in a foreign land and made something of themselves is a source of gratification I feel that cannot be matched.

Going through the entire metamorphosis of maturity and pain with my mother was thought-provoking, to say the least. I now have a deep and profound level of admiration for her that is unparalleled. Prior to hearing the details of their lives, I had already respected my parents greatly, but to know the pain, the trouble and the triumphs that they have experienced makes their story something truly wonderful to experience and share. In my opinion, my parents are examples of what can happen if you only just believe in yourself.

Believing in yourself can take you quite a distance, and I now feel that this is what drove my parents along the journey that took them to where they are today. Shame is not a characteristic that someone who believes in themselves typically displays. Yet, even as my mother believed in herself, she was ashamed of her disease and all that she endured because of it. She was ashamed of limitations that she perceived she had due to the disease, and she was ashamed of her appearance, which was brought on by the changes the disease made her undergo. But, as with all other fights that she faced in her life, she was able to defeat that shame and wear her victory over rheumatoid arthritis as a badge of honor.

I said in the beginning that I grudgingly took on the task of helping my mother write her memoirs, because of my perception of the nature of the relationship that we share. Not only am I glad that I took on this task alongside her, but I now feel that it was critical that I did so. I have learned about the people my parents are. I have learned where they came from and about all of their struggles. I have learned about my mother's pain and her suffering. I have learned of her battles that she refuses to lose with a disease. I have learned that she is probably the toughest fighter that I have ever known, and, consequently in my eyes, she is the greatest mother.

I am glad that I helped her with this project because, by learning who my parents are, I now have a greater sense of who I am. By virtue of this project, I have a new-found respect and admiration for my mom as a person, as a physician, but most of all as my mother. I have added many complex layers to my initial view of her, and, not surprisingly, she continues to peel those layers back. This book gave me the vehicle to begin this voyage of discovery, and for that I thank her.

I think her story is an inspiration for all women, as well as all people who suffer from chronic diseases. But, for me, she is an inspiration simply because she is my mother, and somehow she always was able to put on a smile and pretend that the world revolved around me. She has always been there for me, even when it literally hurt. Thank you Mom, I love you.

Danny Miller

www.ingramcontent.com/pod-product-compliance
Lightning Source LLC
LaVergne TN
LVHW041810060526
838201LV00046B/1198